Founded Upon A Rock

Dr. Dale E. Young

For Eddie & Elizabeth Hodges
Thanks for faithfully
serving God
Dale E. Young
Room 8:28

Copyright 2016

By

Dr. Dale Edwards Young

ISBN **978-1-940609-56-0**

Soft cover

All rights reserved

No part of this book may be reproduced or transmitted in any form or by any means, electronic or mechanical, including photocopying, recording, or by any information storage and retrieval system, without permission in writing from the copyright owner.

This book was printed in the United States of America.

To order additional copies of this book contact:

Dr. Dale E. Young
13074 Turtle Creek Pkwy
Gulfport, MS 39503

FWB Publications
Columbus, Ohio

ACKNOWLEDGEMENTS

Dr. J. Milton Henry (deceased), Professor of History, Austin Peay State University, suggested the topic for a thesis. His suggestions and guidance were valuable in pursuing the work. The thesis was proofread by Linda P. Darrell and Rick Rasberry (now Dr. Rasberry at Liberty University).

William Henry Oliver gave many hours for personal interviews, correspondence and access to letters, papers, books and notes from speeches and sermons to help write the original work. Without his cooperation and assistance, the thesis which became <u>Founded Upon A Rock</u> would have been impossible.

Thanks also to Dr. Herbert C. Gabhart (deceased), President of Belmont University, and Dr. L.C. Johnson (deceased), President of Free Will Baptist Bible College (now Welch College) for taking time from busy schedules for personal interviews.

Thanks goes to Gary F. Barefoot, Librarian at Mt. Olive College, to Judy Shrewsbury, Librarian at Free Will Baptist Bible College, and Helen Desorcy, Metropolitan Board of Education Office at the time when the original work was written.

Deep gratitude goes to my parents (deceased) and sister who had the patience and understanding to allow me to finish the thesis which Randall House published as <u>Founded Upon A Rock</u>.

I never thought about a reprint of the book although I had thought about the years Mr. Oliver lived after I wrote my thesis. Jewell Painter, a graduate of East Nashville High School, met Pat Michols, native of Stewart County, who told her about the book. Thus, began the work which culminated in this edition. Joanna Blackwell, editor of *The Eagle*, the alumni's publication, and Corinne Wright invited me to the East Nashville High Alumni Lunch Bunch. They along with other former students of East provided stories which are noted. Thanks to Eddie, my husband, for assisting with scanning photos and other technical matters that sometimes baffle me! And yes, for putting up with me while I wrote! Carol Reid, librarian at Welch College, was most helpful. Gary Barefoot, Curator of the FWB Historical Collection/University Archives in Moye Library at the University Of Mt. Olive, assisted me once again. Thanks, Nancy Henthorne for proofreading the work. If I've omitted anyone, take it as oversight, not neglect.

Dr. Dale E. Young, Author of this book, (October, 2015) on the porch of Davidson Hall where she lived as a Freshman at Free Will Baptist Bible College.

Table of Contents

Chapter 1   The Foundation is Laid, 1903-1926 9

Chapter 2   Beginning to Build, 1926-1930 39

Chapter 3   The March of a Christian Soldier, 1923-1991 .. 53

Chapter 4   The Largest Sector is Built, 1930-1957 81

Chapter 5   Seven Years at the Helm, 1957-1964 119

Chapter 6   The Apex, 1964-1991 159

Chapter 7   Afterglow 191

Chapter 1

THE FOUNDATION IS LAID

(1903-1926)

William Henry Oliver was born on November 4, 1903, in Indian Mound, Tennessee. Indian Mound is a small village in Stewart County, about twelve miles from the county seat of Dover. His parents were James Harrison (Jimmy) and Frances Lavonia Hembree Oliver. He was named William for his grandfather William Harrison Oliver, and Henry for his uncle, Henry Oliver.

James Harrison Oliver was born on April 6, 1882, near Cadiz, Kentucky. His parents were William Harrison and Susan Litchfield Oliver. They moved to Tennessee when James was about two years old. J.H. Oliver's father was a very versatile person—a carpenter, timber man, farmer and even a writer of poetry. His mother was a homemaker who was especially fond of flowers. This couple had eleven children, ten of whom lived to adulthood. They were very devout Christians. Like most Southerners after the Civil War, they were poor, hard-working people. The Olivers are buried in Hayes Cemetery in Stewart County, near the Montgomery County line.

Frances Lavonia Hembree was born on October 23, 1884, near Liberty, Tennessee. She was the youngest of six children born to David Anderson Hembree and Ephelda Hembree. Having been a little mountain girl, Frances knew the old ballads and most of the wild flowers, which she loved very much. Her parents moved from East Tennessee to Middle Tennessee when she was about thirteen years old, residing in both Montgomery and Stewart Counties. Her parents were also devout Christians with some musical ability. Her father was a Civil War veteran, probably on the side of the North, since he was an East Tennessean. This family was of pioneer stock. The Hembrees lived in Missouri for a time, which was then rather wild. The Hembrees are buried in the Moreland Graveyard, an old Cherokee graveyard, near Indian Mound. No one is buried there except the Morelands and William Henry Oliver's maternal grandparents. (Henry Oliver to the author, July 5 and 24, 1974) Henry's Mother's family were special friends of the Morelands. While Mrs. Oliver was living, the family went around Memorial Day each year to clean off the graveyard and have a service. They always found the graveyard already clean because the younger Morelands kept it clean. At another place, there will be more about the Morelands. (On Mr. Oliver's 84th birthday, he gave his grand nieces and nephews a booklet with wonderful memories, hereafter referred to as "84th Birthday," p. 41)

James Harrison and Frances Lavonia Hembree Oliver had seven children. William Henry was the first born. John Anderson Oliver was born on May 12, 1906. He resided in Nashville, Tennessee where he devoted many years to education in that city. Dovie Frances was born on March 1, 1908 and died from whooping cough on April 8, 1908. (Henry Oliver to the author, August 6, 1974) James Herschel was born November 18, 1910. He lived on a farm in Robertson County near Springfield, Tennessee. Myrtle Mae was born August 27, 1914. She and her husband, Eddis Stanley, lived in the Sango Community near Clarksville, Tennessee. Bessie Pearl was born February 1, 1917, married Henry Bates Miller, and lived in Nashville, Tennessee. Ruby Bernice was the youngest, born December 23, 1919. She died from an accidental rifle wound.

The Olivers lived in a house owned by Dr. J. B. Lahiff when Henry was born. The house was near a site locally known as the A.C. Moore home on Rooster Street in Indian Mound. In 2015, Katheryn Richardson lived there. Shortly after his birth, they moved to a house on the T.W. Seay farm near Indian Mound where John was born.

Little Henry's first memory dated back to about the time of John's birth. He remembered seeing a cow jump over a paling fence to get to her young calf. Included in his early memories were those of his first school days. The Olivers lived near Dick's Fork, which was "up the hollow" from what is today the Indian Mound United Methodist Church. He started to school at Indian Mound in 1909 in a building which is now the Masonic Hall (photo at end of chapter). Henry's father was proud of his oldest son as he took him to school that first day. He did not accompany him later, but he usually sent his son in the care of one of the neighbors. Hayden McGregor was a faithful companion to little Henry. Later, Hayden's younger sister, Clarice, also accompanied Henry to school. For a time, the Olivers lived on the Wilson Farm near the Rories. The Rorie children and William Daley proved to be friends who could watch out for Henry. This was the era of the one-room school when one walked to school with no concern about busing. William Henry's first teacher was Mrs. Fonnie (Sally) Spiceland. Indian Mound had two teachers that year. Mr. and Mrs. Fonnie Spiceland both taught and he was the principal. Little Henry did not have a seat of his own that first year as little first graders sat with the big girls way back in the room. When Henry tried to be creative by drawing, his teacher thought he was wasting time since that was before the day when teachers looked for creative children. Even in those days there was "individualized instruction." During this time, each student was at work on his studies while the teacher went around the room to help any individual who needed it. Henry remembered one day when this was in progress. All was quiet. Henry had to sneeze and, as was his custom, he said "scat" afterwards. Fortunately, no disciplinary action was taken on this little fellow who had disturbed the quiet of an individualized learning center. Thus began what was to be the polestar, the consuming interest of William Henry Oliver—education.

The years of 1910 and 1911 were filled with events that would stand out in the mind of Henry Oliver for years to come. Herschel was born in 1910 while the Olivers lived on the Wilson Farm. Sometime during the year, they moved to the Flem Smith Place which was a little closer to Indian Mound. Henry was all of seven years old now. The house on the Smith Place had running water on the back porch. It was piped from a spring which was located a short distance up a hollow from the house. This was of real interest, for Henry had never seen anything like it before. In 1911, Henry began that great sport of fishing. He could always make hooks out of straight pins and look forward to using real fishing hooks when his Uncle Bill Hembree came. On his walk to school, Henry had to cross Dick's Fork Creek twice. The old timers said it was ten degrees below zero that winter. Henry slipped and fell into the icy waters of the creek. Half-frozen and crying, he finally reached the school. Some of the big girls rubbed snow on his hands, the prescribed remedy to keep cold hands from hurting. It would take more than this to keep Henry from school, although he had thoughts of going home that day. School was out for the year at Christmas time. Henry and his friends and relatives enjoyed firecrackers that Christmas. Young Henry wanted to attend school for more than the five-month term. There was a subscription school with tuition of one dollar per month. J.H. Oliver wanted Henry to attend also; however, there was one hindrance. He did not have the dollar. Thus, Henry and most of the children in the community put school aside until the next fall.

J.H. Oliver had been a sharecropper, preacher and maker of cross ties. Now he decided to invest in some farming equipment and rent a farm. He and his family rented and moved to the Cherry Farm in Cherry Hollow, later known as the Lewis Farm. To those from Indian Mound, it is remembered as the Everette Grizzard Place, located on Highway 46, between Red Top on Highway 79 and Indian Mound. Henry's father bought mules and necessary farm implements. He paid $150 a year to rent about 150 acres. The Olivers lived there about three years. J.H. Oliver's parents and two of his brothers, Alfred and Porter, lived on the farm, too. Eventually, another brother, Billy, came to the Cherry Farm. He died with tuberculosis, leaving six children for his parents to raise. Money was tight due to three dry years. Hard worker though he was, J.H. could not get ahead on his rented farm. In 1913, ten-year-old Henry learned to plow. The mules didn't pay attention to Henry's "Whoa," so he set about to find something that they would heed. The magic word proved to be "Wee." One could see a small boy of ten plowing on the Cherry Farm using "Wee" as he commanded his mules to halt.

The Olivers were as close to the McGregor School now as they were to Indian Mound. Having no school zoning laws, they chose to attend McGregor. The school building was fairly new and named for Manson McGregor, a leader in the community and school board member who wanted a good school in his community. The building served as a meeting house for Sunday School on the first day of the week. McGregor School burned years ago, but the old cistern was still on the site in the 1970s. As you drive from Indian Mound on Highway 46 toward Highway 79, you turn right about a half mile past the Cross Creek Baptist Church. You can only come within a half mile of the old school site as no road leads up the hill to the site. Back in the 1970s, Henry and others who attended McGregor could still spot trees they climbed. Was that really the hum of recitation? No, it was only memory's imagination of days long ago. (Henry Oliver to the author, July 5, 24 and August 6, 1974) The school was in a wooded area, with many large stumps scattered on the school ground. Do you hear the bell calling students to class? That bell was mounted on a stump. Furnishings included desks designed for two pupils and recitation benches near the stage where classes recited various lessons. Drinking water came from a cistern with a pump. Pupils all used the same dipper to dip water from a large bucket. That is until a teacher decided that was unsanitary and said each child needed a collapsible tin drinking cup. Some parents couldn't afford ten cents for the cup. Henry had two little sweethearts, letting each of them think she was the only one. School hours were from 8:00 to

4:00. Going to pick persimmons was one "field trip." ("84th Birthday," pp. 1, 15)

No longer did Henry walk to school by himself. His brother, John, now walked with him. Iron ore had been taken from pits in many parts of Stewart County. The Oliver boys went near several abandoned pits as they journeyed to McGregor School. Henry and John were walking calmly along one morning when they suddenly heard a frightening noise, apparently coming from one of those pits. Was it a bear? Was it a wolf? The boys' hearts beat faster and faster! The nearest way to school lay right by where that noise originated. The two boys ran all the way home, never stopping to think that the noise could have been only a stray dog. What that noise was remains a childhood mystery. It was enough to cause Henry and John to go back to Indian Mound to school, walking a well-beaten path. (Henry Oliver to the author, July 5, 1974)

Herschel Moreland was about Henry's age but did not attend McGregor School because he was not white. He walked several miles over the Montgomery County line to attend a Negro school. Henry felt strongly that this was not right. Herschel was a Cherokee whose family had migrated to Stewart County about 1820. They had escaped the horrible "Trail of Tears." They were people of considerable culture, high morals and integrity. In previous generations, the Morelands were homeschooled years before it became common among some groups. They had their own church, shop and mill. Around 1947, Henry heard Manny say with pride that for 125 years there had not been an arrest in the family, nor an illegitimate child. Herschel and Henry had a wrestling match before a wheat-threshing crowd. Herschel demonstrated his superior strength in the first round and Henry did not ask for a second. (84th Birthday, pp. 39-40)

Dogs were always special to Henry Oliver. Jack Mann, as Hayden was called, and his four brothers lived with their uncle, Manson McGregor. Jack and Henry were about the same age. Jack had a collie named Grundy which Henry described as the finest specimen of his breed he had ever seen. As an adult, Henry saw beautiful collies at the American Kennel Club; so this was quite a statement. He acquired his first very own dog at the age of nine when the family lived on the Cherry Farm. It was a black and tan English shepherd named Shep. Grundy was in lots of dog fights but only one with Shep. Grundy gave Shep a quick thrashing. Jack always said Grundy fought after all teeth were gone. Henry said, "Even the greatest of dogs, and men, grow old." Henry's stories, sermons and lectures often contained his beloved dog stories. He tells several stories about another dog, "Old Shep." Henry had the measles at the time he saw this dog bleeding to death and he fainted at the sight. They buried "Old Shep" in a deep grave and watched to be sure no animals bothered the grave. He named these other dogs: Keno, Dixie, Rock and Ruff. His friend Pete had a two-dog team that pulled his wagon. (84th Birthday pp. 8, 9, 12, 74) One must conclude that Henry loved dogs!

After three years on the Cherry Farm, the Olivers moved again. They moved to the Wright Moreland Property which was near the present Cross Creek Baptist Church but didn't live there long. The Morelands owned the land and the Olivers were sharecroppers. Henry's Uncle Alfred Oliver's second marriage influenced the Olivers' next move. Alfred married a widow, Mary Bryant, but they soon separated. Alfred continued to live on her farm in Montgomery County, not far from Red Top, where Highway 46 intersects Highway 79. The J.H. Oliver Family moved there to farm. This land is now part of the Fort Campbell Military Base. It was near Clinard's Store. (Henry Oliver to the author, July 5, 1974)

Henry Oliver recalled some memorable events during the year in Montgomery County. He began shooting a gun. His father had bought a breech-loader from Bill Hembree for three dollars. Henry and John took turns shooting it when they went hunting. Of course, each boy needed a gun. They bought a muzzle-loader for one dollar. When Henry was not working on the farm, he helped Tom Vaughn with his tobacco crop. At a nickel an hour, he could make fifty cents a day which would buy a box of shells or a twenty-four pound bag of flour. John only made three cents an hour because he was younger. These wages were greater than the pennies their father paid for catching tobacco worms. The year was not all work as Henry did go to school at Plain View School. The only thing he recalled from that year was a yell the teacher taught. It went like this:

Re mo ri!

Ke mo ki!

Polly wants a zigzag!

Polly wants a ki me!

Sis boom bah!

Plain View! Plain View!

Rah! Rah! Rah!

Henry had long forgotten the name of the teacher.

    None of these events were the most important ones of Henry's twelfth year. It was during this year that he read the Bible through for the first time and also became a Christian. (Henry Oliver to the author, September 21, 1974) When Henry was seven, he told his father on his way to a cousin's funeral that he intended to become a Christian when he was twelve. He knew that was the age of Jesus when He said He must be about His Father's business. By his twelfth birthday, Henry developed a reluctance to the idea and decided to wait as close to his thirteenth birthday as possible. He stated, "I can hardly explain this reluctance except by assuming that Satan was working in my mind to keep me away from Christ as long as possible. This is Satan's business." He attended a revival at the blacksmith shop at Needmore in the summer of 1916. Located in Montgomery County, Needmore is on Lylewood Road, between Highway 79 and the Cumberland River where the ferry crosses to Cumberland City. Henry's father and Bill Hembree were preaching. Henry said, "I think that Dad was preaching the night of my conversion." An inner voice seemed to tell him it was time; he went to the altar, followed by his younger brother, Johnny. There was no longer any reluctance. The altar was a small, cleared area in front of the improvised pulpit, covered with sawdust. His father counseled him, speaking of repenting and asking for forgiveness. Yet, Henry felt he needed to do something else. "Dad said that I should say in my prayers, 'Lord, take me and do whatever You will with me.' This was complete surrender of my life to God . . ." After that prayer, Henry was satisfied. He and Johnny received joyous congratulatory handshakes and hugs from their parents and friends. A day or two later he gave his first testimony, choking and speaking with difficulty. Yes, the

Holy Spirit convicted young Henry that night, and he believed on the Lord Jesus Christ as his personal Savior. Soon after his salvation, he was baptized in nearby Blooming Grove Creek by his father. He then joined Dunbar's Chapel Free Will Baptist Church, which had been dedicated in May of 1914. (84th Birthday, pp. 76-79) The church was full in those days with wagon loads of young people coming to the services. Henry recalled many times when he had to sit on the edge of the platform as all the pews were filled with adults. (Henry Oliver in a sermon "One Great Gathering" at Dunbar's Chapel, July 28 1974)

The Olivers moved back to Stewart County after a year in adjoining Montgomery County, returning to the Moreland Place and McGregor School. The school grounds knew no boundaries. Pupils sometimes played in shallow water of a nearby pond or skated on the ice in winter. The West Gibbs Pond, north of the school, was the largest one in the area, covering two or three acres. The pond probably resulted from digging iron ore before the Civil War. There were no compulsory attendance laws; attendance was irregular. The school had students in grades one through eight. Teachers gave much homework. Henry usually did homework by the light from a coal oil (kerosene) lamp; oil cost five cents a gallon. He recalled one time when he worked by moonlight because they had no coal oil. (84th Birthday, pp. 6, 50) Miss Virgie Butts (later Mrs. Angers Seay), Miss Clarice Tucker and Miss Hattie Wallace (later Mrs. Robertson) were three of the young ladies who taught at McGregor. Mrs. Robertson came to Dunbar's when Henry preached at homecomings in the1970s and 1980s. Any teacher appreciates seeing students who have succeeded in life. McGregor was evidently considered one of the least desirable positions in the county. More than knowledge of

subject matter and professional ability was needed to teach there. The enrollment was approximately sixty students with as few as four attending on days of inclement weather. The teacher's salary was thirty dollars a month; ten dollars of that went for room and board. Miss Butts received a raise, bringing her salary to thirty-two dollars. One must certainly say, "Hats off to those girls who taught there." One year, they tried three teachers before they found the one who would stay at McGregor. (Henry Oliver to the author, July 5 and August 6, 1974)

There were two events that Henry clearly recalled from these years. In December of 1918, there was about eighteen inches of snow on the ground on Monday morning. Drifts along the rail fences were much deeper. Henry and John started to school as usual because they never missed. The wind was strong and cold; the boys couldn't follow the customary path. It was tough going, especially for Johnny. He was a strong little fellow and when Henry got across the cornfield, he was right with him, as always. They went through the woods and finally reached Manson McGregor's home. The teacher boarded there and she informed the boys that there would be no school that day. So they went rabbit hunting. The other event was the flu epidemic. All the family had the flu at the same time, except for Johnny. He was only twelve years old, but he did the cooking. He hitched up a mule and snaked saplings from the woods so the family was kept warm. Johnny's work probably saved the lives of the immediate family. (84th Birthday, pp.24, 25)

The students at McGregor hardly lacked amusement. Students enjoyed games like "Two-Eyed Cat" and "Fox in the Morning, Goose in the Evening." Catching mice was their most enjoyable sport. Mice were usually found between the outer and inner layers of bark on stumps on the grounds. Yes, boys brought mice inside to amuse the young ladies! Cattails grew around a pond near the school. There was nothing like blowing cattails into the air. The boys visited a cave down on the bluff. Henry and Pete Terrell halted one expedition to the cave because Pete was scared that a bear might appear. (Henry Oliver to the author, July 5, 1974) Boys at McGregor enjoyed shooting pop guns with dogwood berries for ammunition. The gun was a cylinder of cane or alder bush about six inches long. A ramrod, preferably made of tough hickory, was about three inches long. A boy who could make a good gun was respected. Compressed air propelled the ammunition out of the cylinder and the filling of the vacuum created the popping sound. While nobody was hurt in their wars, the guns popped and hurled the berries several yards. Fights among the boys were frequent, but Henry didn't fight much because he knew his teacher frowned on it and his father had advised him not to fight unless there was a very good reason. On one occasion, he decided he had a good reason. Clint Holiday was picking on Johnny. Henry told him to pick on someone nearer his size, meaning himself. They went into the woods to settle the matter. Henry had Clint flat on his back after a hard scuffle. Henry whipped his opponent in a "fair fight." Henry was proud of his speed and accuracy in throwing rocks, another pastime. (84th Birthday, pp.19-21, 33)

During the early years of Henry's life, the Olivers did what most families in the Indian Mound area did to provide for basic needs. Henry described how to make lye soap, hominy, maple syrup and crossties. The family earned money from making crossties. Crossties are the heavy timbers underlying the steel rails on which wheels of a train roll. Henry said his father and his brothers were the best tie hackers in the community. A tie hacker was one who hewed ties in the woods. Making crossties and hauling them to the river was the main way of earning cash. Ten cents per tie was the going rate with the same pay for hauling them to the river. Henry and his father made ties but didn't haul these. Henry began helping his father when he was twelve; on his sixteenth birthday, Mr. Oliver made twenty crossties while Henry made ten from start to finish.

> One of the most treasured of my boyhood memories is a vivid mental picture of my father and I sitting on a smooth buck cut facing each other eating the meal that Mother had prepared for us. ...We thanked God before eating. Surrounded by the peaceful quiet of the forest, broken occasionally by the singing of a bird or the cawing of a crow, with good wholesome food and hearty appetites, healthy and happy bodies and minds, we had a most enjoyable feast.

This is Henry's description as he worked with his father. A buck cut was a log big enough for just two crossties. They had hewed both edges of both ties and then split the ties apart. What was left made their table for dinner as they called it. He knew how to hunt ginseng. Henry went fox hunting and squirrel hunting. (84th Birthday, pp. 54-59)

> Corn was the "staff of life." Cornbread was eaten with nearly every meal. Henry described in detail the process of corn from the field to the table. His family always planted white corn. They broke ground with a turning plow and went over it with a harrow. Rows were about three feet apart and the grains of corn were planted about every fifteen inches. To avoid covering up the tiny corn stalks with a plow, they

sometimes used a scratcher called a geewhiz. They owned no tractor, plows were pulled by mules. When harvest time came, mules pulled a wagon between the rows, with a man on each side to break the ears from the stalks and pitch them into the wagon. Corn was stored in the crib. Shucking and shelling followed. Usually, they did not have a corn sheller; there was one in the neighborhood which was passed around. Many times shelling the corn was a family affair, done by hand. They took corn to Furr Vaughn's grist mill in Indian Mound. Henry was usually the first customer of the day. Mr. Vaughn would pay him a nickel to bring two or three buckets of water from Honey Fork Creek to pour into the gas engine to get it started. Grain was poured into a hopper which forced it into the grinder and corn meal was the result. Mr. Vaughn took a scoop of the meal for his pay. (84th Birthday, pp. 45-48)

Henry Oliver took his first trip to Dover, the county seat, when he was twelve. His Uncle Frank Hembree was preaching revival at McGregor School. Some rowdy boys in the community became angry when the preacher called attention to their misconduct during the service. The boys took revenge by assaulting the minister on his way home. Frank had the boys arrested for disturbance of public worship. Since Henry heard the shots, he was called as a witness when the case was tried in Dover. Frank carried a gun for a while afterwards, even to religious services.

It is rather difficult for one to imagine what Indian Mound looked like when Henry was young. Its one real street was lined with businesses. Highway 46 goes through the village by way of what was the street back then. There were four or five stores plus the gristmill.

The Olivers lived for about a year on what was known as Harrison Hill. It was later the site of Jack Ford's home and in the 1970s the site of the Bob Lewis home. Henry got his dog, Keno, when he lived there. He described this dog simply as a wonderful dog. This dog lived from the time Henry was in the seventh or eighth grade until he graduated from college. Flossie Wolfe, Miss Gunson and Grace Coppedge were teachers at Indian Mound during these years.

The house was the second one the Olivers lived in which was owned by the Morelands. An older family of Morelands were their closest neighbors. Henry's family got water from their spring house. Henry described their flower garden as exquisitely beautiful. He sold newspapers which they bought every week. As a minister, he felt honored to hold funerals for several of the Morelands. In 1917, He attended the 100th birthday celebration of one of the original settlers. He conducted the funeral of Mannie and Roberta, parents of Nathaniel (Nate) and Christine Moreland who were the last of the Morelands of Indian Mound, cousins to Henry's friend Herschel. They rented the old home place and lived at Oakwood during their last years. (84th Birthday, pp. 40-41) It was the author's privilege to visit them along with Henry in the 1980s. (Information and pictures of this family are in Stewart County, TN, Vol. II, pp. 77-78)

William Henry Oliver next moved with his family to the Charlie Blane Place. It was about a fourth of a mile from Indian Mound. They lived there about a year. Henry's youngest sister, Ruby, was born in the middle of the night on December 23, 1919. At the age of sixteen, Henry was old enough to go for the doctor. He rode his mule as fast as he could to get Dr. C. N. Keatts, who lived up Dick's Fork. Dr.

Keatts had one of the first automobiles in the area. Thus, he arrived at the Oliver home before Henry got back.

Henry finished the first half of the ninth grade at Indian Mound in December of 1919. The other members of the class were Elva Moore Atkins, Oscar Vaughan and Gilbert Stalls. Their teacher was Mrs. Eunice Coppedge. (Henry Oliver to the author, August 6 and September 21, 1974)

J.H. Oliver was concerned about Henry's education. He decided it might be best for his eldest son to continue his high school education in Dover. Two former Indian Mound residents, sisters of Angers and daughters of Tom Seay, Sr. had moved to Dover when they married. They were Lillian (Mrs. John Bruton) and Lora (Mrs. Harvey Bruton). Henry boarded at Lillian's so he could attend Dover High School. On January 5, 1920, Henry and his father walked about three miles to the Cumberland River and crossed on a ferry at the Cross Creek Landing. By noon, they arrived in the Long Creek community. After having lunch with Mr. and Mrs. Ed Wallace, it took most of the afternoon to walk to Dover. The same trip today takes about fifteen or twenty minutes, but in those days it took the better part of a day.

Arriving at the Brutons, Henry saw the nicest house he had ever seen. It was a two story, white frame house across the street from the Fort Donelson Methodist Church. The house stands no longer but the church is there and still a house of worship. Henry sold a raccoon skin for $4.50 and an opossum skin for $2.25 to Angers Seay in Indian Mound. Henry thought he must have paid top dollar! He purchased his first pair of long pants, other than overalls, for fifty cents from a cousin who had outgrown them. His father had done his part by selling a calf for $11. So the ninety-nine pound, sixteen year old arrived in Dover to further his education.

Professor R.E. Gorham was the principal of Dover High School. The first day was certainly a new experience for Henry Oliver. The boys and girls lined up separately and marched into the school. Students had an hour for lunch. Henry made a wrong turn when he started to the Brutons, but he managed to find his way in time for lunch. Dover High School was a white frame building which became B and M Furniture Store later. (Pictured in Stewart County, TN, Vol. II. p. 33) The building no longer stands; it was near where the First Baptist Church Activity building is. Although Henry had purchased a pair of long pants, he wore them only the first day. He went back to his usual knee length pants and long stockings.

Henry's education continued for more than one month. When his father came to pay his room and board, the Brutons would not take his money. Henry worked around the house and in Bruton's Drug Store on Saturdays in return for room and board. This business later operated as Bruton and Webb Drugs. (Pictured in Stewart County, TN, Vol. I. pp. 489, 523) It was on the east side of what is now Spring Street. The Brutons treated Henry as one of the family. During the summers, he worked in the drugstore for $25 a month plus room and board. He continued his studies in the summers and was able to finish high school in three years. Henry enjoyed school and always made good grades. (Henry Oliver to the author, July 5 and August 6, 1974) Henry Oliver attended both the Methodist and Christian churches while living in Dover. He attended prayer meeting on Thursday night at a mission with the Brutons. At one of those meetings, he awoke to hear Mr. Bruton call on someone else to pray "because Henry's asleep." He did not attend after that as he was usually tired from studying and prone to fall asleep when he was still. (Henry Oliver to the author, July 24, 1974)

During his senior year, Henry was the chairman of the first Stewart County Historical Committee. The chairman of the Tennessee State Historical Committee, John Trotwood Moore, notified Henry of his appointment. "You have been made chairman of your County Committee, the personnel of which is as follows: Prof. R.E. Gorham, W.C. Howell, Hon. N.A. Link, L.S. McElroy, J.T. Reynolds, Hon. Joe W. George, and H.H. Bruton." Senate Bill Number 164 provided for such committees to collect county records "to be preserved forever for the inspection of future generations . . . ." (John Trotwood Moore to Henry Oliver, June 22, 1921, William Henry Oliver Collection, Nashville, Tennessee. Hereafter cited as the Oliver Collection) The Stewart County Historical Committee was organized on July 21, 1921. L.S. McElroy of Dover was the secretary. (Henry Oliver to John T. Moore, June 22, 1921, Oliver Collection) This committee chose five sites to be marked in Stewart County for their historical significance. The sites were Fort Donelson, Fort Henry, Forrest's Crossing, Grant's Headquarters and the Gunboat Landing. (Henry Oliver to the author, August 14, 1974)

Dover High School opened its doors in 1917. The first graduating class in 1921 had four graduates. The faculty had four teachers through the twenties. One teacher during those days was Mr. Oakley Shelby. In 1949, Dover High School became Stewart County High School when the facilities were moved to a brick structure on Spring Street. (Dixie Parker Gorham, "History of Dover High School and Stewart County High School, 1917-1971" printed by the

Alumni Association of Stewart County High School, 1971, in Dover, Tennessee) That building no longer stands; it was located where the Dover Middle School is now.

Twelve graduates comprised the 1922 Class of Dover High School. They were: Emmie D. Joiner, Elva Moore, Helen Brandon, Lydia Brandon, George Brandon, "Judge" Brandon (uncertainty about his real name exists), Ezra Goforth, Rena Lancaster, Lewis Rumfelt, Corinne Marlow, Katie Lee Thompson and William Henry Oliver. "We did not have a valedictorian and the students were not ranked. Unofficially, my rank was either one or two . . . . There was never any official averaging of grades." (Henry Oliver to the author, July 24, 1974) Elected representatives, then as now, sent letters of congratulations to graduates. Joseph W. Byrnes, Congressman from the Sixth District, received an announcement of the commencement exercises from Henry Oliver. He sent "a heart full of good wishes for you in your every undertaking . . . ." Henry. (Joseph W. Byrnes to Henry Oliver, May 17, 1922, Oliver Collection) The *Stewart-Houston Times* (October 12, 1983) ran of picture of the Class of 1922 provided by Henry Oliver. The picture was made following a reception given by Bruton Drug Company.

Henry Oliver returned to Dover many times for the annual Alumni Association's Banquet. He told David Ross, editor of the *Stewart-Houston Times* (date unknown) that he received a "pretty good" education in Stewart County. "I didn't have any problems competing with college students when I left here," he said. "I really love coming back to Dover. I learned a great deal here."

In the meantime, J.H. Oliver had continued his own education. During 1921, he attended school in Indian Mound. He moved to Dover and graduated from the eighth grade in 1922, the same year his eldest son graduated from high school. He passed the teacher's exam and received a teacher's certificate. J.H. Oliver contacted the superintendent of schools in Montgomery County, A.W. Jobe, and he secured a position at the Briarwood School. Thus, the Oliver Family moved from Stewart County to Montgomery County in the fall of 1922. They lived slightly up the Cumberland River from Clarksville, as it was then. They occupied a large brick house on a bluff near the south end of the Cunningham Bridge. That bridge was built during this time. (Henry Oliver to the author, September 21, 1974)

J.H. Oliver enrolled Henry at Southwestern Presbyterian University in Clarksville where Austin Peay State University is now located. Dr. Charles Diehl was the college president. J.H. Oliver asked if there were any special instructions for Henry. Dr. Diehl recommended that he wear long pants. Here was a young man who had graduated from high school in knee length pants, part of a suit the Brutons had graciously given him. Henry's father bought his son a new suit with long pants so that his son might enter college appropriately dressed. (Henry Oliver to the author, July 5, 1974) What a contrast to present day dress codes on college campuses!

Henry Oliver entered college in the fall of 1922 and lived at home with his family. He returned to Dover to work in the drugstore in the summer of 1923. He gave this account of a boat ride from Clarksville to Dover. "I left Clarksville yesterday about 12:00 and reached Dover about 6 p.m. . . . I had a big time coming down on the boat. I steered the boat myself.... I got off at Lock C and stayed a little while." (Letter from Henry Oliver to Herschel Oliver, June 20, 1923, Oliver Collection) Lock C was on the Cumberland River at Cumberland City. Lock D was at Dover. These locks were blown up once the dam was built on the Cumberland River. Lake Barkley was formed at that time. There are pictures of Lock D in <u>Stewart County, TN</u>, Vol. II, pp. 21,549. During the summer, Henry was the superintendent of the Sunday School at First Christian Church where he preached his first sermon. In appreciation of his work, the people gave him a pair of gold initialed cuff links at the end of the summer.

Time came for Henry's return to college. His father was teaching at Shady Grove and had moved to that community. Henry and his brother, John, lived in the house the family had occupied the year before. John attended Clarksville High School. The boys had only one bike. One left early enough to reach his destination by walking. The other washed dishes, cleaned house and rode the bike into town. John fell on the railroad track when he was walking one day and was struck by an oncoming train. This ended the boys "batching." They moved into Clarksville with Aunt Eliza Daley. (Henry Oliver to the author, July 5, 1974)

William Henry Oliver needed financial assistance to continue his education. "The Free Will Baptist Educational-Orphanage Campaign of Tennessee" loaned him some money. J.L. Welch was the president of the organization, G.W. Fambrough the secretary-treasurer and W.B. Davenport the financial agent. The Board of Education consisted of J.L. Welch, J.E. Hudgens, G.W. Fambrough, J.H. Oliver and G.T. Harris. On September 8, 1923, Henry received $100 from this organization. Brother Fambrough gave him these words of admonition. "All a boy has to do is to get the will power and push his case. It all is worth the price. Set your mark high and go to it." On November 27, 1923, the organization sent Henry another check for $150. The next time Henry requested money, there was none available. Brother Fambrough was sorry:

> We have been collecting both the Educational and Orphanage funds together, and have been keeping funds together and several have been subscribing and paying exclusively to the Orphanage funds and a few days ago the Ladies Aid called for their part of the funds and it nearly left us blank for the present. (Letter from G.W. Fambrough to Henry Oliver, September 8, 1923, Oliver Collection)

Henry had seemingly reached an impossible hurdle.

Henry took his finals at the end of the first semester thinking that he would soon be leaving college. Upon his completion of high school, he had received a teacher's certificate in both Latin and English. It was time to use it, or so he thought, as no money was available for that second semester's tuition. "I was trying to prepare myself to teach ministers and other church workers at our Free Will Baptist college, Eureka, in Ayden, N.C." God knew that was Henry's goal. He received a check via mail for $100 from G.W. Fambrough, who did not know how badly Henry needed the money. This was a gift—not a loan. (Henry Oliver to the author, July 5 and 24 1974) Henry's education was not to be interrupted.

On March 14, 1924, G.W. Fambrough sent Henry $25, another loan from the Educational-Orphanage fund. This letter was on Fambrough's stationery. He was a dealer in "general merchandise, garden and field seeds." Seven days later, he mailed Henry $35 to buy a new suit. Apparently, this was a gift. He wrote, "If you go out before our people they will expect you to be neatly dressed." (Letters from G.W. Fambrough to Henry Oliver, March 14 and 21, 1924, Oliver Collection)

Henry's parents wanted to help their son financially.

Son, it makes us both feel sad to know that you need money and we are not able to give it you, but I think there will be some way prepared for us if we do our part and put our trust in the Lord . . . . yes, son, I know that God will care for us and I know that He has cared for us through the past and I believe He will continue to care for us if we will only trust Him. (Letter from Mrs. J.H. Oliver to Henry Oliver, March 12, 1924, Oliver Collection)

Is there any better way to show that the Olivers gave Henry something more vital than money? Trust in the Lord was to see him through life's rough spots long after those godly parents had gone to be with the Lord.

Henry Oliver went to Dover for graduation in 1924. He was the only graduate from Dover High School in college at the time. Professor Gorham asked him to speak to the graduates and to present the diplomas. In the audience sat "Grandma Bruton" listening proudly as Henry spoke. At her side, one of his favorite dogs, Ole John Craig, heard that familiar voice. The dog ran and leaped onto the stage to greet a friend come home. It took some effort to remove the dog so that the program could continue.

At the end of his second year in college, Henry received an appointment to West Point from Joseph W.

Byrnes. (Henry Oliver to the author, August 6, 1974) Immediately, he began receiving letters from various preparatory schools seeking to get him to enroll so that he would pass the entrance exam. Among these were: the National Preparatory Academy, Cornwall-on-Hudson, New York; Marion Institute in Marion, Alabama; and the U.S. Hall West Point-Annapolis Coaching School in Columbia, Missouri. The latter exerted the most outstanding means of persuasion. That school included material from U. Sebree, Rear Admiral U.S. Navy; E.H. Crowder, Judge Advocate General of the War Department; and John J. Pershing, Commander in Chief of the American Expeditionary Forces. These men praised U.S. Hall for the excellent work he was doing as president of the school. (Material from U.S. Hall to Henry Oliver, September 22, 1924, Oliver Collection) All efforts were in vain, however, as Henry Oliver did not accept his appointment to West Point. He was preparing for the work he knew God had for him to do and he saw no point in going to West Point. The Adjutant General, Major General Robert C. Davis, sent Henry Oliver a letter.

> The receipt of your letter of November 5, declining appointment as a candidate for the Military Academy is acknowledged. Accordingly, your conditional appointment as principal candidate from the sixth Congressional district of Tennessee has been cancelled on the records of the Department. (Letter from Robert C. Davis to Henry Oliver, November 11, 1924, Oliver Collection)

William Henry Oliver spent the summer of 1924 in evangelistic work. He was also President of the State Convention of the Free Will Baptist League. During his last two years of college, he served as the first pastor of East

Nashville Free Will Baptist Church. His Christian work is mentioned here simply for the sake of chronology. The details are chronicled in a later chapter.

Time had come for Oliver to change colleges. He attended George Peabody College during the summer of 1925 because Vanderbilt would not give him credit for the two years of Bible he took at Southwestern. In the fall, he entered Vanderbilt University. (Henry Oliver to the author, July 24, 1974) There he had the famous Fugitive poet who encouraged his writing abilities. Oliver wrote literature and poetry, composing the well-received poem titled *At Twilight*. This poem is the epilogue in Stewart County, TN, Vol. II and also appears at the end of this chapter with his signature. "The best teacher I ever had was John Crow Ransom at Vanderbilt. I had composition and criticism under Mr. Ransom. He was very kind and concerned, and he read and graded carefully every paper he asked you to turn in. (Renee Elder Vaughn, "East High's Oliver knew his calling from the start," *The Tennessean*, November 3, 1986)

He lived in the home of Mrs. Fannie Polston at 318 Woodland Street who was a leader in the East Nashville Church. He lived in Kissam Hall at Vanderbilt part of his senior year. Henry graduated from Vanderbilt in the spring of 1926 with a triple major in Latin, Greek and English. In addition, he had education courses which essentially constituted another major. Three sisters gave Henry a Bible for graduation which he was still using when he celebrated his 70th birthday. His rank in class was not especially high as he was the pastor of the East Nashville Church. "This affected my grades in college. I have never regretted this, however. The work at East Nashville was important." Henry Oliver to the author, August 14, 1974)

At Twilight

At twilight one may feel himself a part
Of everything that's pleasing to the soul;
Or one may feel that Nature's boundless whole
Is drawn by mystic cords to his own heart,
Or his own self. And nature will impart
To man's poor soul a portion of her own
Rich beauty. And a sleeping heart of stone
May waken, soften; and, within, may start
Anew the soul-life which heartless world
Of cold realities has crushed to death.
The springs of memory begin to flow
Afresh. And from the heart the weights are hurled
Which long have pinned the struggling soul beneath
Their massive tons. And so the soul may grow.

8-2-87
BAM

The Masonic Hall in Indian Mound, Tennessee. A part of this building was where Henry Oliver started to school in 1909. He came to speak to the Masons here many years later.

This iron bridge was about a quarter of a mile from the Masonic Hall. The photo was made in 1983 but the bridge was built between 1915 and 1925. Thus, Henry Oliver crossed this bridge many times.

Dr. Dale E. Young | 37
Founded Upon A Rock

Iron bridge in Indian Mound, 1927. The tall white building was the T.W. Seay & Son General Store and the small building was the office of Dr. C.N. Keatts. Flooding in the area was common until the dam was built on the Cumberland River in the 1960s. Both bridges pictured were replaced with concrete bridges. Photo came from Ruby Peacher (deceased) and now is in the author's collection.

Chapter 2

BEGINNING TO BUILD

(1926-1930)

William Henry Oliver spent the summer of 1926 in evangelistic work, which will be covered in another chapter. Oliver also spent time trying to find a teaching position for the fall. He considered Battleground Academy in Franklin, Tennessee, Trevecca College in Nashville and various public schools.

Beginning in the fall of 1926, Henry Oliver taught English and Latin at Jere Baxter High School in the Inglewood section of Nashville. His salary for that year was $130 a month. In addition to teaching, he coached girls' basketball and boys' football and baseball. His comment on his first day as a teacher holds a sobering thought. "Today I began my career as a school teacher. I am reminded of . . . Today we launch. Where shall we anchor?" (Henry Oliver to Ethel Walker, September 1, 1926, Oliver Collection.)

During this year, Henry was again living with his brother, John, in a dormitory at Trevecca where John was a student.

In the spring of 1927, Henry received a letter from R.B. Spencer, President of Eureka College in Ayden, North Carolina. He extended an offer for Henry to coach and teach Latin and Greek at Eureka for the next term, which Henry accepted. Henry Oliver began graduate courses at George Peabody College in the summer of 1927. However, he dropped out before the summer ended to do evangelistic work. He did not finish or receive credit for any of those summer courses. (Henry Oliver to the author, July 5, August 14 and October 24, 1974.)

In order to provide some background, here is a thumbnail sketch of Eureka College. A Free Will Baptist Seminary was founded in 1896 with its first building completed in 1898. Free Will Baptists began a college campaign in 1920. Eureka was founded on September 8, 1925; the buildings were occupied on the same date. The purpose of the school was to offer orthodox instruction in line with the Bible for ministers, missionaries, Sunday School superintendents and teachers, and those intending to engage in church auxiliary work. Other denominations were invited to send students to Eureka. Eureka had a high school and a two year college program offering courses in Bible, church history, doctrine, and missions. The college offered other courses related to church work. ("Eureka College," *The Free Will Baptist*, XLIV, August 8, 1928, 10)

"Rev. William Henry Oliver of Nashville, Tennessee will teach science and coach athletics." ("Eureka College News," *The Free Will Baptist*, XL, August 24, 1927, 6) Not enough students were interested in Greek for it to be offered, and he didn't teach Latin because it was necessary for him to teach the math and English classes. He also coached boys' and girls' basketball and boys' football. Furthermore, Mr. Oliver directed a music group and taught "Rudiments of Music" in the evenings. Although he did not feel well qualified in music, he had done a little work like this for Mrs. Eva Thompson Jones, his voice teacher in Nashville, and on WDAD, a radio station. "I guess my teaching was better than nothing." Eureka paid Mr. Oliver $150 a month for his services. Though the work was neither what the first offer was nor what was published, young Oliver knew Eureka was where the Lord wanted him in the fall of 1927. He had realized a dream to which he had prepared himself. (Henry Oliver to the author, July 5 and October 24, 1974.)

When you move to a new place, first opinions are interesting. Henry wrote home and said that Eureka was not much of a school, but he gave ample hope that it would become a great one. Eureka had about sixty-nine students and eight teachers. The administration building was good enough for "Peabody or Vanderbilt, far better than anything at S.P.U." The work done was good. The foremost point was the place Oliver thought Eureka should take in the Free Will Baptist denomination. "If the FWB denomination fails to support Eureka . . . I think that the entire church should be absorbed by other churches . . . . It seems that this is the time God has planned for a nationwide FWB awakening. If we fail to wake now, we ought to sleep forever." (Henry Oliver to Rev. J.H. Oliver, September 13, 1927, Oliver Collection) This chapter finishes the story of Eureka, but not of Free Will Baptists. Nearly a half century later, Oliver again wrote on education and this denomination.

Henry's duties in North Carolina included more than just what he did at Eureka. He had "some church work convenient to Ayden." President Spencer found it gratifying to find a young man who was willing "to serve in a double capacity." (R.B. Spencer, "Eureka College," *The Free Will Baptist*, XL, August 31, 1927, 4) Rev. Oliver preached at the North Carolina State Convention on "Christian Duty" based on Christ's words to Peter, "Feed My Sheep." At that convention, President Spencer gave a forceful address on what Eureka College really was. ("The Recent State Convention," *The Free Will Baptist*, XLIV, September 21, 1927, 8) Professor Oliver preached in Kinston at least once. (College Reporter, "Eureka" *The Free Will Baptist*, XLIV, October 5, 1927, 11) In the spring of 1928, he used his music ability. The Woman's Auxiliary Convention of the Central Conference met on March 28, 1928 at Spring Branch in Greene County. Special music was "directed by Rev. W.H. Oliver of Eureka College." ("Auxiliary Convention of the Central Conference," *The Free Will Baptist*, XLIV, March 7, 1928, 10) Since he was the reporter for the college, his duties included writing for *The Free Will Baptist*. (Henry Oliver to Rev. J.L. Welch, October 11, 1927, Oliver Collection) Henry was a member of the Eureka College male quartet, which sang at many churches in Eastern North Carolina. A highlight for the quartet was when they sang at a Billy Sunday Revival in 1928. Other members of the quartet were R.E. Tripp (North Carolina), J.R. Davidson (Georgia) and I.J. Blackwelder (Florida). (Henry Oliver to the author, February 23, 1975)

Rev. Oliver actively promoted Eureka in his home state. He was elated when his church in East Nashville was among the first to respond to a request for supplies for the college. "September 19 the express agent here at Ayden announced that a large box had made a successful journey all the way from Nashville . . . . ("Eureka," *The Free Will Baptist,* XLIV (September 18, 1927, 9) Rev. Oliver attended the Cumberland Association's Ministers Conference at Cofer's Chapel in Nashville on December 28, 1927. The chairman was Rev. J.L. Welch. Rev. Oliver made an interesting talk. ("Cumberland, Tenn., Association Ministers Conference," *The Free Will Baptist*, XLIV, January 18, 1928, 5) Professor Oliver and D.B. Sasser left for Tennessee on February 10, 1928, arriving in Nashville the next night. They visited several rural churches in their "four day drive for Eureka." These included Bethel, Brandon's Chapel, Mt. Zion, Oakwood, Rock Springs and Shady Grove. G.W. Fambrough was on the list of contributors to the college. They received $222 on this drive. (D.B. Sasser, "Our Tennessee Trip," *The Free Will Baptist*, XLIV, May 2, 1928, 13) In the spring, the Bethlehem Ladies Aid in Cheatham County sent food to Eureka. The Heads Church in Robertson County sent food, "including a ham of meat." (Henry Oliver, "Eureka," *The Free Will Baptist*, XLIV, May 2 1928, 7) Is it little wonder that a Tennessean delivered the baccalaureate address at Eureka? Rev. J.L. Welch spoke on May 27, 1928. "Rev. Welch . . . has been secured as speaker . . . and those who know Mr. Welch can assure you that his message will be inspiring and uplifting." (Henry Oliver, "Commencement Notice!," *The Free Will Baptist*, XLIV, May 9, 1928, 7) Graduation ended the 1927-1928 term at Eureka.

Though it seemed Henry was completely absorbed in his work, he found time to think of love. True, he had written, "I seem to be looking . . . not for love, but for a life of service." (Henry Oliver to Catherine Trotter, April 29, 1926, Oliver Collection) He put God first and trusted Him to take care of the details. If it was God's will for him to love and marry, God would provide the right one. He corresponded with and dated many girls over the years. He stated that no one could have asked for a nicer group of girlfriends than he had. Then, he met the one who took the "place of all of them and then some." (Henry Oliver to the author, November 29, 1974)

Henry met Pauline McCall at Heads Church in the summer of 1926 where he was conducting a revival and she was visiting country cousins. As he approached the church for the eleven o'clock service, he heard someone playing the piano. The music was far superior to what he had been hearing. When he entered the church, the two were introduced, but there was no romance for several months. John dated her for a while before Henry did. (Henry Oliver to the author, October 24 1974)

Pauline was the only child of Mr. and Mrs. Albert Bruce McCall. Mr. McCall was a victim of the flu epidemic of 1918. The McCalls, professional people, were among the original settlers of Smith County. With more than ordinary culture and refinement, Mrs. McCall was the former Mattie Haynes. The Haynes family were road builders, engineers and construction workers who had little interest in formal education.

Pauline graduated at the head of her class of about 400 at Hume-Fogg in 1927. After graduation, she took a business and secretarial course at Fall's Business College, finishing with honors and a teacher's certificate. She was very talented in music, especially in piano and organ. (Henry Oliver to the author, July 25 1974)

"Dad, Pauline and I are planning to be married next June, if I can get your consent and Mother's . . . . I love

Pauline,--I'm willing to stake my life on the proposition-- and I want her with me." (Henry Oliver to Rev. J.H. Oliver, October 16, 1927, Oliver Collection)

The sunrise of May 22, 1928 shed its glow on the newlyweds, Mr. and Mrs. Henry Oliver. The couple married at her home in a "sunrise wedding" ceremony attended by a few close friends and performed about six o'clock by his father. Mrs. Eva Thompson Jones and Mr. Joe Carnbron sang, accompanied by Miss Amanda Cunn. The couple left immediately for North Carolina. One of Pauline's friends took them to Murfreesboro in a Packard, where they met Rev. J.L. Welch. These three and Herschel Oliver went to Ayden in his Ford. Of Pauline, Henry said, "What a girl!" What she gave up to become my wife! We really went through some rough times together, but she never complained. She loved me." (Henry Oliver to the author, October 24, 1974)

The Olivers were in Ayden for graduation at Eureka. ". . . There is Prof. and Rev. W.H. Oliver. He has since his stay with us this year won the hearts, not only of our own people, but the entire community . . . . He is a worker . . . interested in the cause of the Master and yet free from ostentation. He wins by his humble Christian walk." ("Commencement at Eureka," *The Free Will Baptist*, XLIV, June 6, 1928, 9)

Henry and Pauline spent the summer of 1928 in North Carolina. He did evangelistic work, mostly by using his music for God's glory. He also hauled barn wood in a Reo speed wagon for twenty-five cents an hour. He worked as a carpenter's helper for Mr. E.W. Braxton for the same wages. (Henry Oliver to the author, February 23, 1975)

William Henry Oliver was listed as the principal of the high school and instructor in mathematics for Eureka in the fall of 1928. ("Eureka," *The Free Will Baptist,* XLIV (September 18, 1927, 9) He was living in his third home since arriving in Ayden, having lived in the boys' dormitory the first year. He and Pauline had a room with Mr. and Mrs. E.W. Braxton; his third home was a rented, furnished house in Ayden. Mrs. McCall, Pauline's mother, lived with the Olivers. She was in charge of the food program at Eureka when the fall term began. (Henry Oliver to the author, October 24, 1974) This lady continued to support Bro. Oliver's ministry for the rest of her life. The author remembers her coming to Dunbar's Chapel with him in the 1950s. Professor Oliver did more than just teach for the college. "W.H. Oliver, Director of Vocal Union" is listed under "Election of Officers." He sang in a quartet and rendered a "very impressive solo, "The Lost Sheep" at the same meeting. ("Union Meeting," *The Free Will Baptist,* XLIV, December 5, 1928, 10-11)

Eureka sought for but never attained a secure financial base. The struggle for survival was valiant but it was destined for defeat.

> Due to the lack of funds . . . the High School Department has been indefinitely suspended. The Bible Department, however, through the courtesy and favor of Rev. L.R. Ennis, will operate through the spring months without cost to the school. This is made possible by the unsalaried services of Brother Ennis. ("Eureka College High School Suspended," *The Free Will Baptist,* XLIV, January 9, 1929, 12)

Various attempts were made to secure sufficient funds to prevent "indefinitely suspended" from becoming permanently closed. W.G. Asher solicited the support of ministers. While he wasn't a Free Will Baptist, he was a "sympathetic outsider." He believed that if ministers had God's work at heart that the people could be led in real giving to the Lord. (W.G. Asher, untitled article, *The Free Will Baptist*, XLIV, January 2, 1929, 4) The ladies of the Little Rock Church of the Western Conference in North Carolina called the women to arms. "To our minds the loss of Eureka College means the death of our denomination. Can't we women save it?" (Mrs. Wiley Lamm and Mrs. E.F. Phillips, "A Call to the Women of the F.W.B. Denomination," *The Free Will Baptist*, XLIV, February 13, 1929, 10) The sad answer coming from posterity was no because Eureka permanently closed. The administration/classroom building later burned. (Henry Oliver to the author, August 6, 1974) The boys' dormitory was still standing in the 1970s as a private residence which had undergone several changes. The curtain came down on Eureka's role in the drama of a denomination. Would it be the final act of the Free Will Baptists as several predicted? Henry Oliver said that the stream of Free Will Baptist education simply flowed underground when Eureka closed. (Henry Oliver, "Flowing and Growing," *Free Will Baptist Bible College Bulletin*, March/April, 1971, 1) God, in His providence, gave the Free Will Baptists another golden opportunity to flow as a mighty river. That opportunity continued as Christian young people were trained at Free Will Baptist Bible College (now Welch College). These young people have gone forth to make a mark for Christ, generation after generation.

The closing of Eureka brought real disappointment to young Henry Oliver. Funds were not available to pay his salary. He took an old typewriter and a violin as partial compensation. A student had given these to Eureka for tuition because the student had no money. With the typewriter, violin, his wife, a heavy heart and shattered dreams, Oliver returned to Nashville. Forty-one years later he became a part of the main stream of Free Will Baptist education again.

On December 10, 1929, Henry became a salesman for the National Life and Accident Insurance Company. He did not especially enjoy the work because he felt that he was persuading people to buy something they really didn't want. His health was not good; he took his doctor's advice to quit the job and travel. The travel came in a rather unique way. He sold candy, papers, magazines and drinks to passengers on trains that traveled to Atlanta and St. Louis. Such a person was known as a newsboy on streets, but on trains one was called a news butch. The railway employees addressed these boys as "Butch." Henry met interesting people and enjoyed the travel, too.

By the end of the summer, Henry Oliver was able to resume his work as a teacher in Cheatham County. He was the principal of Kingston Springs and taught all seven high school classes. The school had five teachers and ten grades. His salary was $150 a month. (Henry Oliver to the author, July 5 and 25, 1974) Mr. Oliver boarded with Mr. And Mrs. Alton Mayes in this town located about twenty miles from Nashville. In those days, schools enjoyed wonderful support from the citizens. During the year, electric lights were installed in the school. Mr. Oliver coached boys' and girls' basketball. Both teams won most of their games, and the boys won the county championship. Mr. Oliver enjoyed the year at Kingston Springs for personal reasons as well as for the accomplishments made at the school. "There were fields and forests and streams a plenty and I did a lot of hunting and hiking and rambling through fields and woods. Sometimes I hunted for Indian arrowheads in the fields." He regained his health completely which had been impaired by disappointment, illness and overwork. Pauline usually came for him on Friday afternoons, and he stayed in Nashville until Sunday afternoon. (Henry Oliver to the author, February 23, 1975)

Administration Building – Eureka College

Boys' Dorm at Eureka College. It still stands in Ayden, NC where it is a private residence, a southern colonial style home.

Dr. Dale E. Young | 51
Founded Upon A Rock

Eureka College students and teachers. The second person from the left on the front row is listed as W. H. Oliver (teacher).

Faculty at Eureka College
Back Row, Left to Right: Henry Oliver, Principal, Robert Tripp, and T.B. Melleete; Front Row, Left to Right: Sarah Brown Braxton, Sarah Wood, and Thelma Moody

Eureka College Quartet, 1927-28. From Left to Right: J.R. Davidson, I.J. Blackwelder, William Henry Oliver, and R. E. Tripp

These photos from Eureka are in the Free Will Baptist Collection, Moye Library, University of Mt. Olive (NC) and were provided by Gary F. Barefoot, Curator, FWB Historical Collection/University Archives.

Chapter 3

THE MARCH OF A CHRISTIAN SOLDIER

(1923-1991)

This chapter attempts to recapture the experiences of William Henry Oliver as he served in the ministry which spanned the years from the time of his first sermon in 1923 until the end of his life. Being a Christian permeated all areas of his life. Yet, for the purpose of this work, it seemed best to devote a separate chapter to his Christian service.

Henry Oliver preached his first sermon at the Christian Church in Dover, Tennessee during the summer of 1923. He preached his first sermon at a Free Will Baptist church in the fall of that year when the Cumberland Association convened at Brandon's Chapel in Bumpus Mills, Tennessee. He devoted the next few summers to evangelistic work.

His first revival was in the summer of 1924 at Emanuel's Chapel in Dickson County, where W.T. Hagwood was the pastor. A number of people were saved in the revival. Bro. Oliver was paid seven dollars for this revival, which was good for the times. He was a licensed minister, not yet ordained. There were eight conversions and seven additions to the Heads Church when he preached there in July of 1924. The next week he was at Oaklawn in Cheatham County assisting Bro. D.T. Armstrong in a meeting. Henry then went home to Clarksville for a week to be with his Dad in a revival at Shady Grove. He preached a revival at the Indian Mound Free Will Baptist Church which no longer exists; it was located across the road from the present Methodist church. T.W. Seay, Jr., who was not a member of the church, gave him five dollars, a super generous contribution for that day. (Henry Oliver to the author, July 5, 1974 and March 13, 1975) On August 24, he was with Bro. W.B. Davenport at New Hope in Cheatham County. (Henry Oliver to Fannie Polston, August 5, 1924, Oliver Collection) He traveled to Ashland City on a train and walked most of the way to New Hope. His text on the first night was Isaiah 53 and there were about twenty decisions that night.

Henry was serving as President of the State Convention of the Free Will Baptist League, the youth organization. Through this work he became acquainted with Free Will Baptists in East Nashville. This group rented the upstairs of an Odd Fellows Hall at Twelfth and Woodland Streets on August 1, 1924. For the next two years, Henry Oliver was their pastor; receiving four dollars a week for his services. During the first year, he still lived in Clarksville and had to ride the train each weekend. If he rode the Tennessee Central, he had fifteen or twenty cents left of his salary. Four dollars was not quite enough to ride the Louisville and Nashville. On the weekends, he stayed in the home of Mr. and Mrs. Fred (Fannie) Polston at 318 Woodland Street. Mrs. Polston was a leader in the East Nashville Church. (Henry Oliver to the author, July 5, 1974)

When the Cumberland Association convened at Oaklawn in October of 1924, Henry Oliver preached the introductory sermon, "Christianity's Conquering March," using Acts 1:8 as his text. He was re-elected as clerk of the association. The Annual Presbytery met at the end of the meeting, electing Rev. D.T. Armstrong as moderator and Rev. J.H. Oliver as clerk of the presbytery. The ordaining council consisted of Rev. J.E. Hudgens, Rev. A.D. Duncan, Rev. J.L. Welch, W.B. Davenport and Bro. G.W. Fambrough. Brothers John W. Boyte and William Henry Oliver were recommended to be ordained to the full work of the ministry. Ordination followed with prayer and the laying on of hands, after which there was a season of great rejoicing. In the same month, the East Nashville Church was organized with nineteen members including their pastor. Average attendance for preaching was forty-five. (Minutes of Cumberland Association of Free Will Baptists, Historical Collection, Moye Library, University of Mt. Olive, Mt. Olive, North Carolina. Also, Welch Library, Welch College, Nashville, Tennessee, October 22-24, 1924, 3-6, 16) The official organizing ceremony was on November 2, 1924 with Bro. Welch in charge. The charter members were:

Mrs. O.C. Briley
Mrs. Curtis Cantrell
Mrs. Irene Polston Coville
Mrs. Eva Drake

Mrs. Dona Layne
Mrs. Fannie Polston
Mrs. J.P. Polston
Miss Candis Puckett
Mrs. Eva Ray
Mr. William D. Ray, Jr.
Mrs. Alexine Black
Mrs. J.B. Smith
Mrs. Joe Smith
Mrs. Ruth Stewart Edmundson
Mrs. Martha Stewart
Mr. D.E. Teasley
Mrs. D.E. Teasley
Mr. Jess Wheeler
(Henry Oliver to the author, July 24, 1974)

Mrs. Polston and Rev. J.L. Welch were perhaps Henry's dearest friends in Nashville at that time. He wrote home that his Nashville friends, especially Bro. Welch and Mrs. Polston, had been extra nice to him. He did not have any money, but Bro. Welch gave him all he needed. "His lessons, and his advice, too are very valuable." Although Mr. Fred Polston wasn't a Christian or church member at that time, he was very good to Henry. One Saturday he bought him a pair of shoes, two shirts, a forty-five dollar suit and a hat. On Sunday night he went to church for the first time in six years. (Henry Oliver to Mr. and Mrs. J.H. Oliver, July 19, 1924 and April 6, 1925, Oliver Collection) "There is an interesting story about Mr. Fred Polston's final illness and conversion . . . I did have the honor and privilege of leading him to Christ, thank the Lord." (Henry Oliver to the author, March 13, 1975) Henry moved to Nashville in June of 1925 where he attended Peabody that summer and enrolled in Vanderbilt in the fall where he graduated in 1926.

East Nashville had twenty-six members by the summer of 1925, some with seemingly almost superhuman energy and zeal. In May, they raised over $225. (Henry Oliver to Alberta Tippit, June 8, 1925, Oliver Collection) It appeared the young pastor had strength and zeal, too. His prayer was to do God's will regardless and for a closer spiritual walk with God. Crowds were sometimes slim but God does not bless according to numbers. "Only 19 at church tonight, but the service was good. All Christians after the service seeking fuller consecration. Two at altar wishing to be reclaimed, one hand raised wishing conversion." (Henry Oliver to Catherine Trotter, June 9, 1925, Oliver Collection)

Henry Oliver worked with Bro. Welch, the pastor of Cofer's Chapel in North Nashville, that summer, too. "I am conducting the singing for Bro. Welch's revival at Cofer's Chapel. There were about 6 conversions last night. (Henry Oliver to Rev. J.H. Oliver, June 17, 1925, Oliver Collection) This was only one of many times these two soldiers of the cross would be on the field together fighting God's battles. On July 15, 1925, Henry held prayer meeting at Cofer's Chapel although he had three exams the next day. (Henry Oliver to Mrs. J.H. Oliver, July 15, 1925, Oliver Collection)

Bro. Oliver had a revival at Brandon's Chapel in Bumpus Mills in September of 1925 with Bro. D.T. Armstrong. The problems an evangelist encounters weighed heavily on him at the time, making him feel weak for the responsibilities he had to assume. "Please pray that God may help me to preach the way of salvation in such a way that the people will understand. There was only one profession last night although three more came forward for prayer." (Henry Oliver to Charlie Mai Swan, September 1, 1925, Oliver

Collection) Later that month, Henry went to direct the song services and to render special music in Ashland City where Bro. Welch was in a revival. (Henry Oliver to Alberta Tippit September 21, 1925, Oliver Collection) The Ku Klux Klan had a delegation there on Saturday night, clothed in their hoods and robes. At their request, Henry sang one of their songs, "The Bright Fiery Cross." (Henry Oliver to Ethel Walker, October 4, 1925, Oliver Collection)

And what did they do for church socials then? The League at East Nashville had a "'possum hunt" on November 19, 1925. About forty people, including the pastor, had a good time, but they caught only one 'possum.

Henry Oliver remained a member of East Nashville Free Will Baptist until his death in 1991 and was a part of its work throughout. The congregation purchased the building at 518 Woodland Street from the Woodland Street Christian Church in November, 1929, and had their first service in that building on May 11, 1930. Rev. Oliver was present for the groundbreaking of the present building which was completed in 1965. Henry Oliver served as chairman of the "Golden Anniversary" Committee and wrote "A Note Concerning Our Music" giving some of the history of music in the church. His sharp wit and obvious love for the church and his Lord was a blessing to all when he spoke at the anniversary celebration. (East Nashville Free Will Baptist Church, *Golden Memory Book*, pp. 1,4-5,14-16,18) This church now is the Five Points Fellowship, a Free Will Baptist community, located at 210 S. 10th Street.

Henry Oliver engaged in evangelistic work in the summer of 1926. In July, he walked ten or twelve miles of the way to Oakwood Free Will Baptist near Cedar Hill.

(Henry Oliver to Catherine Trotter, November 20, 1925 and July 20, 1926, Oliver Collection) The next week he preached at Dunbar's Chapel near Indian Mound where there were eight decisions for salvation on August 4. During the week, he stayed with Mr. and Mrs. John Summers, Sr. (Henry Oliver to Alberta Tippit, August 5, 1926, Oliver Collection)

Henry Oliver was the pastor of Bethel in Cheatham County from 1925-1927 where he only preached on the second Sunday of each month. The church address was Neptune, Tennessee, located about fifteen miles from Ashland City. Many times John Oliver filled his brother's pulpit at East Nashville on these Sundays. (Henry Oliver to Ethel Walker, December 15, 1925, Oliver Collection)

The young minister not only served as a pastor and preached in various churches; he was involved in almost all the Free Will Baptist work in his area and participated in state activities as well. The Tennessee State Convention of Sunday Schools met at Bethel on May 29, 1927. Bro. L.O. Burroughs was secretary of Sunday Schools and Bro. Oliver was elected recording secretary and treasurer. (G.W. Fambrough, "State Sunday School Convention of Tennessee," *The Free Will Baptist*, XL, June 15, 1927, 12) A few months later he published "Suggestive Notes for Sunday School Board, U.S. Conference." He included these suggestions:

1. Unity in the work
2. Gather information about every Free Will Baptist Sunday School possible
3. Pastors organize and encourage the Sunday School
4. Improve the literature used

5. Train the teachers
6. Build Sunday School rooms
7. Promote the Sunday School by speeches and written articles in *The Free Will Baptist*

(Henry Oliver, "Suggestive Notes for S.S. Board, U.S. Conference," *The Free Will Baptist,* XLIV, November 2, 1927, 14)

It is noteworthy that some of these were emphasized years later in the denomination.

The Seventh Annual Convention of the Ladies Aid Society met during the first week of August, 1929, at Rock Springs near Neptune, Tennessee. Henry Oliver gave "A splendid address on Temperance" the first day. (Mrs. W.D. Ray, "Annual Convention of Ladies Aid Society in Tenn.," *The Free Will Baptist,* XL, August 24, 1927, 11) This is another example of his varied activities.

Never did the young man forget his Christian parents and the significant role they played in his life. He wrote to his mother, "I know you wish you had a chance to do more. Well, whatever I do, a large share of the credit belongs to you and Dad." (Henry Oliver to Mrs. J.H. Oliver, March 20, 1926, Oliver Collection)

Henry Oliver moved to Ayden, North Carolina in the fall of 1927. He resigned as pastor of Bethel Church to join the faculty at Eureka College. On October 9, 1927 he was elected without opposition as pastor of the Ayden Church, where the pastoral board recommended him and the former pastor favored him. His annual salary was about $800. (Henry Oliver to Rev. J.H. Oliver, October 9, 1927, Oliver Collection) He attended the 1928 meeting of the General

Conference of Free Will Baptists when convened in Ayden. This was a forerunner of the National Association of Free Will Baptists. Young Oliver served as chairman of the Education Committee and made a brief report at that meeting. (Henry Oliver to the author, May 1, 1975) Henry Oliver's work in North Carolina has been documented in chapter two. One remark from those years is significant. He wrote the following on his twenty-fourth birthday to his Grandfather Oliver.

> You are 56 years older than I. The line of Christian service has been unbroken for 120 years, you say. If I can live to be 80 years old and can work from now until then, the line will have been unbroken for 176 years . . . I'm glad to do my part . . . God has been good to me . . . I want to serve Him to the best of my ability. (Henry Oliver to Rev. W.H. Oliver, Sr., November 4, 1927, Oliver Collection)

Since Henry lived to be eighty-seven, the chain was unbroken for 183 years.

When Henry Oliver returned to Tennessee he resumed his active role in Free Will Baptists' circles there. So we focus on those years.

In 1930, the Cumberland Association voted unanimously to begin an institute to train Christian workers. They met at the East Nashville Church. J.L. Welch was the first director and Henry Oliver was his assistant. The minutes of the 1931 meeting contain a report of this institute. Attendance at this meeting in January was low but some accomplishments were noted. Courses studied included Homiletics, Sunday Schools, Leagues, Ladies Aid, Church

Administration, Music and Helps in English. The teachers were Mrs. J.E. Frazier, Rev. and Mrs. J.L. Welch, Mrs. Fred Polston, Mr. Burnett, Mr. Madison Waggoner and Rev. Henry Oliver. "On motion Rev. Henry Oliver was elected Supervisor of the quarterly meeting. . . On motion Rev. W.H. Oliver be reimbursed for his services." (Minutes of Cumberland Association, October 22-24, 1930, 4; October 14-16, 1931, 9; October 17-19, 1934, 7) Thus began Rev. Oliver's work to organize the Cumberland Association's churches into districts for quarterly conferences.

Meeting in Ashland City on December 1, 1934, Rev. Oliver announced that three districts were formed. These districts were:

> Western Group: Brandon's Chapel, Dunbar's Chapel, Gorman, Pleasant Hill, Scott's Chapel, Union Hill. W.R. Carroll was elected chairman of this group.

> Central Group: New Hope, Ashland City, Miller's Chapel, Bethel, Mt. Zion, Bethlehem, Oak Grove, Emanuel, Friendship Chapel, Oaklawn, Good Springs, Oakwood, Hagwood Chapel, Olivet, Heads, Rock Springs, Shady Grove. W.B. Davenport was elected chairman of this group.

> Eastern Group: Cofer's Chapel, Craigfield, East Nashville, 1st FWB Church of Columbia, Fredonia, Mt. Pleasant, Oakland, Spring Hill, Starky's Chapel, West Nashville. J.H. Oliver was elected chairman of this group. (Minutes of Cumberland Association, October 16-18, 1935, 13)

As the chairman of the Western Group, Rev. W.R. Carroll corresponded with Rev. Oliver on at least two occasions. Rev. Carroll wrote Rev. Oliver that he would do his best to get the churches together on Saturday, July 25, 1935. He requested that Rev. Oliver make out a program and preach the 11:00 sermon. Rev. Oliver had asked Rev. Carroll to assist in a revival at Bethlehem to which Rev. Carroll replied, "Will be more than glad to help you and will be there on that date if the Lord's willing. So let us pray for a great revival." Rev. Carroll had not decided on the host church but he thought Dunbar's Chapel would be best because it was nearer for the people living on the south side of the Cumberland River. This letter was signed "Fraternally Yours, W.R. Carroll." (W.R. Carroll to Henry Oliver, May 16, 1935)

Rev. Oliver remained the supervisor of the quarterly meeting in 1936. Rev. Carroll again wrote for the Western Group in response to a card from Rev. Oliver. He stated it would be alright with me for you to have conference at Dunbar's if it is satisfactory with them. (W.R. Carroll to Henry Oliver, September 24, 1936) The report for 1936 summarized Henry Oliver's work. Quarterly meetings had been held regularly in all three districts with a good response from the people. He personally visited fifteen of the Cumberland Association's approximately forty churches. Some recommendations made in his report are still practiced. For example, the minutes should contain a tabulated report of the work of all ministers. This saved space and gave a more complete record. The form to be used was submitted and is still used. The statistical record at the end of this chapter was compiled from these forms. The recommendations did not just remain local but reached out to encompass the entire denomination. "That this association

... inform our National Board of Education and the Free Will Baptist Denomination at large as to ... the attitude of the people of this vicinity ... toward the selection of Nashville as a location for our national school." This report showed the scope of Oliver's interest. He suggested that the association have a Supervisor of Music to promote better singing, that requirements for ordination be strictly adhered to, and that the Board of Education make plans for correspondence courses for the coming year.

At the same associational meeting, a committee was appointed to work to organize the Tennessee Free Will Baptist Convention. W.B. Davenport was the chairman; serving with him were Bro. W.E. Coville and Rev. Henry Oliver. (Minutes of Cumberland Association, October 14-16, 1936, 6, 10-11) It took time to lay the groundwork for this task. It was organized on May 1, 1938 and convened as a body in September. The first Tennessee State Association met at the East Nashville Church with Henry Oliver present to represent his association. The officers were:

George Dunbar, Moderator
J.L. Welch, Assistant Moderator
William Henry Oliver Secretary-Treasurer
G.W. Fambrough, Assistant Secretary-Treasurer

Rev. Oliver was also the chairman of the committee to revise the Constitution and Bylaws. These revisions were made and accepted. Henry Oliver served on the Tennessee Home Missions Board from 1939-1941. In 1948 the association met at New Hope, where Rev. Oliver rendered special music. (Minutes of the Tennessee State Association, September 1, 1938, 1939-1941, 1948)

Henry Oliver had a keen interest and connection with establishing the denomination's school in Nashville. He didn't officially serve on any board or committee which had anything to do with the founding of the school in 1942 which became Free Will Baptist Bible College and is now Welch College, named for Henry Oliver's dear Christian friend, J.L. Welch. Located at 3606 West End Avenue, plans are for Welch College to relocate to Gallatin during the 2016-2017 term. His close friends, Mrs. Polston and Rev. Welch, were the principal representatives of the Cumberland Association involved in starting the school, and Rev. Oliver stayed in close contact with them. They discussed the school and were in agreement in their thinking. All three felt a new school was needed, primarily for training ministers. The school should serve the denomination and be centrally located. Since Nashville was centrally located, in the midst of quite a few Free Will Baptist churches, and was a center of schools, colleges and libraries, the city seemed to be the logical choice. When the time was right to locate in Nashville, the West End property was priced right and located in a good community. "I think God has been leading . . . that He is still doing so and will continue to do so . . . We have many college-trained persons in our denomination; but, at the time plans were being made for our new school, I was about the only one . . . ." (Henry Oliver to the author, May 1, 1975)

From the account of Henry Oliver's work, we see a partial picture of his faithfulness to his God, his churches and his denomination. Faithfulness was a trait of the Olivers for years. In the "Obituaries" of the 1939 minutes it was stated that Rev. J.H. Oliver, Henry's father, had attended twenty-nine of the last thirty associations. Little wonder that "we never had a man that we missed more . . . than dear Bro. Oliver." (Minutes of Cumberland Association, October 11-

13, 1939, 8) J.H. Oliver was known for visiting the sick. On his way home from visiting at a local hospital, he suffered a stroke, made it home and muttered something about "the 14th chapter." He must have been referring to John 14. Soon after, he lapsed into unconsciousness from which he never revived. Dr. Cleo Miller came to the home at no charge. The family put J.H. Oliver in the hospital and he lived three or four days. Rev. J.L. Welch conducted his funeral at Cofer's Chapel. Interment was at the Hayes Graveyard near Needmore in Stewart County where his parents and other family members were buried. Graveside services were attended by people from Stewart County and Nashville. Local men dug the grave as a final tribute to a good man, loved and respected by many. T.W. Seay, Sr., longtime friend and benefactor, stood at the foot of the grave, steadying the casket as it was lowered into the grave. (Henry Oliver to nieces and nephews, date unknown) At the time of his passing, J.H. Oliver was the pastor of Dunbar's Chapel in Stewart County. His son, Henry, faithfully pastored that country church for the next ten years. Both the crowds and offerings were slim. The author's Mother was saved on August 26, 1945 under the ministry of Rev. Oliver. Rev. Oliver was the pastor of Dunbar's Chapel again from 1950-1952. (Henry Oliver to the author, July 5, 1974) He is the first pastor of Dunbar's that the author remembers. He only preached two Sundays each month.

Excerpts from a letter in 1945 show a connection between Dunbar's Chapel and Free Will Baptist Bible College when Rev. Oliver was the pastor.

> The student body of the Free Will Baptist Bible College has engaged in the enterprise of the publication of a College Annual. . . . In addition to

the . . . Annual, there will also be featured a volume of vital information of the whole program of the denomination as represented by the National Association. . . .It is planned that many hundreds of these annuals will be distributed throughout the several states of our connection. It is felt in College circles that every friend of our cause will be proud to possess a copy of this Annual. It is the desire of the students that your church may be represented in the Annual in the form of a compliment consisting of the name of the church, its post office address, and the name of its pastor . . . The charge for this church compliment is $5.00. . . Your church will be furnished a copy of the Annual for the enjoyment, inspiration, and blessing of its members. (Mr. & Mrs. Huey Gower to Henry Oliver, January 17, 1945)

Even during the years when Henry Oliver was employed full time in a public school system, he was involved in church work. For example, he gave the graduation address on May 30, 1957, as the fifteenth year at Free Will Baptist Bible College came to a close. Mr. Oliver was then the principal of East Nashville High School with nearly thirty years of experience as an educator. ("Oliver and Miley Will Speak at Commencement Exercises, *Free Will Baptist Bible College Bulletin,* V, May, 1957, 3)

Henry Oliver had his share of stories to relate about incidents in his years of ministering to various congregations. One day he decided to preach a long sermon at Bethlehem Church. He didn't want to disappoint this congregation who were accustomed to long sermons. According to his watch, he had preached only twenty minutes. He reviewed his sermon simply to learn that he had still spoken only twenty minutes. Yes, his watch had stopped! The moral of this story is "Stop when you're finished regardless of what your watch says." (Henry Oliver, "One Great Gathering" at Dunbar's Chapel, July 28, 1974)

Difficulties arose as he tried to fill preaching appointments. He was provoked during World War II because beer trucks could get gas when he could not. He was then the pastor at Dunbar's Chapel, located about seventy-five miles from Nashville. To reach the church, he sometimes rode the train and Mr. John Summers, Sr. usually met him. Occasionally, they had to use a canoe to cross the backwater on their way to the church. There were days when they got stuck in the mud on Hayes Ridge. Was such to stop the march of this soldier in God's Army? Assuredly not, as he never missed an appointment at Dunbar's Chapel. (Henry Oliver to the author, July 5, 1974)

Retirement at age sixty-five comes to some but this would not be the case for William Henry Oliver. He had not completed his part of the unbroken chain of 176 years of service he had written about to his grandfather in 1927. He became the annual speaker for the homecoming service at Dunbar's Chapel. Many times he talked about loved ones who had gone and been greeted by their Savior with the wonderful words, "Well done, thou good and faithful servant . . ." Ever one to give a special twist to words, he said, "And we who are left to labor . . . we on whom the sun of life still shines may hear the same greeting at the close of our life's day if we are faithful, if we trust and obey." Bro. Oliver reminisced that at sixty years old his hair was almost as white as it was fifty years before when he was a child sitting on the edge of the platform. He had attended the dedication of the church in 1914, and described Bro. Pickel (or Pickle) who had organized the church. Bro. Pickel was a large, white-headed, fat preacher who named ever horse he owned Charley. This preacher loved to tell jokes, but most of all he loved to sing, pray, preach and quote Scripture. Once when Henry's mother was dangerously ill, Bro. Pickel prayed for her in the middle of the night. The Olivers were grateful that God spared her life. Henry Oliver recalled the Cumberland Association's meeting at Dunbar's when most people came in buggies. He remembered revivals, baptizing's in the creek, shouting in services, and singing. The first time Henry remembered coming to Dunbar's, he and his father had dinner with Mr. and Mrs. Ed Brinton. He described their two dogs! A white, bob-tailed dog came to church regularly but laid quietly throughout the services. Bro. Oliver also recounted experiences from his days as pastor. Once the backwater was so high that only one other person attended, both he and this man came part of the way in a canoe. When he asked the church to get someone in his place, it was not because he wanted to leave or was tired. Rather, he felt it was best for this church. "Even from the grave the voices of our friends and loved ones seem to cry out to us, challenging us, begging us, to do our duty, . . . for 'the night cometh when no man can work. . .' Who will take their place?" Yes, the narrow, sometimes dusty, sometimes muddy, roads had been replaced with blacktop. The tall trees in Brigham Hollow and Boat Gunnel were gone. These and many other changes were noted. However, an unsaved person was still lost and God's whosoever was still extended to all. "The Bible is still God's Word and its assurance of God's love and of God's forgiveness remains as sweet and sure and strong as in days gone by. 'Come unto me' Jesus still proclaims. 'all ye that labour and are heavy laden, and I will give you rest. Take my yoke upon you, and learn of me; for I am meek and lowly in heart: and ye shall find rest unto your souls.'" He had the pastor to extend an invitation for the lost to be saved, any Christians to join the church and his Christian friends to pledge continued prayers for each other. There were those in the congregation he had prayed for daily for twenty-five years. ((Henry Oliver, "Homecoming at Dunbar's Chapel," July 26, 1964)

In 1970 he spoke on the many changes that had occurred; in 1971 he preached on "God Doesn't Change." His sermon in 1973 was "God's Judgment." His text was Matthew 25:31-46 in 1974 and he titled his message "One Great Gathering." His message had not changed in fifty years; it was still "Jesus Saves." He didn't fail to call sinners to repentance. "I wish to thank all of you for the check, which your wife called a 'love offering.' You are most generous. You all must love me a lot. . . I love the church and the community and the county very much."

He often visited people in the community when he came to Dunbar's. "I visited Mrs. Milliken on my way to church. I like your pastor." The pastor was Maxie Milliken and the lady mentioned was his mother. (Henry Oliver to Fulton Edwards, July 30, 1974) Sometimes the local paper would carry news about Rev. Oliver's speaking engagements in Stewart County. One listed him as Henry Liver which brought a chuckle to him as well as other readers of the article. Rev. Oliver visited Acree Norfleet in the Veterans Hospital in Nashville. (Henry Oliver to the author, October 18, 1985) Yes, this minister cared for others and took the time to show it even when his own health was failing in his older years. The last time the author heard him preach at Dunbar's Chapel was in 1987. This godly man continued to be a blessing to all those with whom he came in contact.

Ministers regularly officiate at weddings and Rev. Oliver did his share of officiating at these ceremonies. He did this service for many family members, including nieces and nephews. Yes, these weddings included some of his East Nashville High students. Then, there were family members of the author's, including her parents.

At the other end of the spectrum, ministers conduct funerals. While there is no record of all the funerals Rev. Oliver conducted, it is appropriate to note his words comforted many over decades. He conducted Harvey Bruton's funeral from the front porch of his home in Dover in 1945. The casket was covered with a wreath of daisies and other wild flowers from the fields, a tribute to Mr. Bruton's love of nature. "In front of me lay the family Bible, man's surest source of wisdom, strength and comfort." Rev. Oliver used Psalm 1, 90, and 23 as well as John 14. He would use these passages on many other occasions. Henry Oliver heard a redbird singing throughout the service and after the benediction, stated, "And the redbird was still singing in the dogwood tree in the valley." (Harvey Bruton's Funeral, Oliver Collection) As the pastor of Dunbar's Chapel, he conducted services for both the author's grandparents, Rena Brinton Dunaway (1949) and William R. Dunaway (1951). Rev. Oliver comforted the author's family at funerals for four of the Dunaway's children, Matt (1961), Jimmy (1976), Taft (1984), and Maggie D. Norfleet (1986). The last comforting words the author heard him say were at her Daddy's funeral on December 7, 1986. Rev. Oliver had planned to attend the 40th anniversary celebration of Fulton and Ophelia (Dunaway) Edwards but sadly, he was in Dover that day for the funeral of a World War II veteran forty-five years after Pearl Harbor was bombed. In January, 1989, Henry Oliver attended the funeral of his schoolmate and lifelong friend, Jack Mann, but he was unable to speak due to his failing health. (Obituaries and personal memories of the author) In customary Oliver style, he wrote, "Please tell your mother that I appreciated the note that I had from the family following Taft's funeral. It was an honor to be wanted. I expressed the thanks of the family to the young lady who drove for me. She was pleased." (Henry Oliver to the author, September 2, 1984) "I considered it an honor to be asked to hold your Aunt Maggie's funeral. She was a great lady, and the 31st chapter of Proverbs was indeed appropriate." (Henry Oliver to the author, October 31, 1986) Although the author doesn't have such notes he wrote to others, knowing how thoughtful, humble and appreciative he was, he wrote many such notes.

As an older gentleman, Henry Oliver reminisced about his zeal as a young man who wanted others to be saved.

> I sometimes fear that my zeal for the salvation of lost souls is not as warm or strong as it was. ... God forgive me, if this is so. . . I have been active in religious work for many years. I have had a long and full life of teaching, preaching and singing and just living. Through the long, busy years, . . . I have returned in memory many times again to the sawdust altar in the old blacksmith shop at Needmore in the summer of 1916 where I asked God to take me and do whatever He pleased with me. There has never been a time when I regretted making the commitment . . . nor has there ever been a moment when I was not willing in my heart for God to do whatever He pleased with me. God has been faithful

and kind. I hope that my life has been lived in accord with His plan for me. ("84th Birthday, pp. 78-79)

The statistical record which follows gives only a glimpse of the life and work of this man of God. Only eternity will reveal what God wrought through the life of this soldier marching under the banner of the cross.

YEAR	Church or Other Ministry	Sermons Preached	Prayer Meetings Conducted	Funerals Conducted	Marriages Performed	Special Services Held	Revivals Conducted	Revivals Assisted In	Conversions Witnessed	Received Into Church	Baptisms Witnessed	Homes Visited	Miles Traveled	Received From Church	Received From Other Sources
1924	East Nashville	125	15					10	140						
1925	East Nashville	108	9	3				6	36	8		20	500	$196.00	$20.00
1926	Bethel														
1927	Ayden, N.C.														
1932	Olivet	87	4	1	1		1	7	67	39	43	86	3,180	$120.00	$183.78
1934	Olivet Bethlehem	76	2	1			2	3	21	16	10	213	3,440	$289.00	$47.69
1947	Dunbar's Chapel	33		1	9		1	1	20	11	11	186	3,000	$180.46	$62.00
1948	Dunbar's Chapel	28		4	7	16	1		11	1	1	100	3,000	$165.83	$70.00
1949	Dunbar's Chapel	35		12	5		1		12	1		100	2,000	$187.12	$60.00
1951		12		3	8				5			50		$65.00	
1955		16	2	3							1	75	2,000		
1961		4	1	1					6			30			
1963		4		1											
1966		10		2	2				10			45			
1967		10		4	4				10			40			
1970	FWBBC	3		6	4				6			50			
1971	FWBBC	9	2	8	4				4			25			
1974	FWBBC	7	1	10	1				4			50			

Source: Cumberland Association Minutes, 1924-1974

Dr. Dale E. Young | 75
Founded Upon A Rock

Rev. and Mrs. J.L. Welch, dear friends of Rev. Oliver, for whom Welch College is named.

Photo from FWB Historical Collection, Welch Library, Welch College

Rev. Henry Oliver officiated at many weddings. This picture is in the parlor of the Oliver Home at 201 South 12th St. As the pastor of Dunbar's Chapel FWB, he performed this ceremony on December 3, 1946. Pictured from left to right are Margaret (Dunaway) Norfleet, Fulton Edwards and Ophelia (Dunaway) Edwards (the author's parents), Beatrice (Dunaway) Mann and Rev. Oliver.

Photo is in the author's collection.

Rev. Henry Oliver at Dunbar's Chapel FWB
in the early 1950s.
Photo from Dorothy (Elliott) Bryant

Rev. Henry Oliver at Dunbar's Chapel FWB in May of 1979
Photo from Dorothy (Elliott) Bryant

East Nashville FWB Church, 518 Woodland St. 1930-1964
Photo from the FWB Historical Collection, Welch Library, Welch College

East Nashville FWB Church now is Five Points Fellowship, 210 South 10th St.
Photo from Corinne Wright

Chapter 4

THE LARGEST SECTOR IS BUILT

(1930-1957)

When the curtain rose in the fall of 1930, William Henry Oliver was back in the city that was becoming home, Nashville, Tennessee. Despite the fact that there were four vacancies and 400 applicants that year at Hume-Fogg High School, he was hired with a salary of $140 a month. He taught English and Algebra. He coached the baseball team in the spring of 1931, leading them to the city championship. For his coaching he was paid an extra $25 a month. During one season he coached boxing and was the assistant football coach. "I received no extra pay from the Board of Education for this."

The current shifted Mr. Oliver to still another school in September, 1932, which was the newly completed East Nashville High School near his home in East Nashville. In the beginning, he taught English and Algebra but dropped the latter after a short time. (Henry Oliver to the author, July 5, 1974) By then he had enough experience to draw the maximum salary in the system, $170 a month. (Henry Oliver to the author, July 25, 1975) When students arrived early, they sang under Mr. Oliver's direction in the auditorium. Professor J.J. Keyes was East's principal at that time. Shortly after going to East, Mr. Oliver became the Activities Manager which was almost equivalent to being an assistant principal. He was paid an extra $30 a month for duties performed in this capacity. It was certainly true that he was the principal's right hand man. East High was originally built to accommodate 1200 students. The East Junior High addition was constructed in 1937, bringing the total capacity to 1700 students. After Professor Keyes died in December, 1936, W.P. Fisher became the high school principal while H.S. Lipscomb became the principal of the newly opened junior high. Henry Oliver was the registrar, or assistant principal, of East High until 1939 when Mr. Fisher retired. Mr. Oliver became the acting principal at that time and then a year later he became the principal. He remained the principal for seventeen years until he took another step in 1957.

It is appropriate here to bring the history of this school up to the present. East High closed in 1988. It reopened as East Literature Magnet in 1993 a "school within a school" on the campus of East Middle which had been East Junior High. The Magnet Literature School became a "stand-along" school in 1997. Grades nine through twelve were in the high school building and grades five through eight were in the middle school building. In the fall of 2010, East Literature Magnet became a Paideia school which emphasizes critical thinking, problem solving, and civil dialogue. East Nashville Magnet School became the official name in May of 2012. East Nashville Magnet High School will expand and utilize both buildings on the East Nashville Campus in the fall of 2016. The middle school will move to the current Bailey Middle School. (Principal Steve Ball, February 22, 2016)

Just what kind of principal was William Henry Oliver? One way to determine the answer is to share what the students at East Nashville High said. Mr. Oliver urged his staff not to teach citizenship but to instill citizenship in their students. Tandy Wilson, a member of the Class of 1942, said "Mr. Oliver has always been a Christian gentleman and he expected you to be the same. He didn't have to paddle you – he could just look at you. If you saw disappointment in his eyes, that was enough.... He was always there when you needed a friend, and still is." Tandy was a Metro councilman in the 1980s. "Mr. Oliver was more than a school principal. He was a friend to the students and a personal counselor to most of us," said Eddie Jones executive vice president of the Nashville Area Chamber of Commerce in 1986. Eddie said that "Other than my parents, Mr. Oliver had the greatest influence on my formative years of any person I knew." Richard Fulton, mayor of Nashville in the 1980s, was Oliver's student. "I knew Dick very well ... he was a 'B' student. He was outstanding on the football field . . . He was very popular and ran for student body president. . . . He was beaten by George Cates." George was an attorney and was vice mayor before 1986. Joe Clifton, member of the Class of 1943, owned Clifton General Tire Company. He remembered Mr. Oliver's even-handed treatment of problems, including disciplinary problems. "He would talk to us and we understood what he was talking about rather clearly. He was very good at communicating with students, a perfect gentleman at all times and always in control. His method of dealing with people was wonderful." (Renee Elder Vaughn, "East High's Oliver knew his calling from the start," *The Tennessean*, November 3, 1986) Speaking of discipline, here is a most interesting commentary. When Mr. Oliver resorted to corporal punishment, he inflicted on himself the same licks he gave the student—"just to see what it felt like. I believe in kindness, smoothness and congeniality. It doesn't make an iron bar less strong to wrap it in velvet. That's what I always said." He considered it a challenge and an opportunity when he got a student who had been expelled from another school. ("Former East High Principal Oliver Dies," *Nashville Banner*, May 16, 1991)

Henry Oliver was the kind of educator who didn't forget students after graduation. Mr. Oliver came and sat on the front row for a 1976 bicentennial musical play written and directed by Corinne Ford Wright at DuPont High. After the program, "A Tale of Two Centuries," he told Corinne he had never heard so many wonderful songs in such a short time. Later, he asked Corinne's parents "Aren't you glad you made the sacrifice to give her piano lessons?" Mr. Oliver frequently encouraged and congratulated former students on accomplishments. Corinne, chairman of the social studies department at DuPont Senior High, earned the distinction as a fellow to Taft Seminar II in Washington, D.C. through the American University in 1983. He sent her a copy of "Taft Institute taps two here for creative teaching" from the Metro Schools NEWS and VIEWS. His handwritten note said, ". . . Congratulations! I have many graduates that I am very proud of—doctors, lawyers, musicians, ministers, etc. I am proud of them. I want you to know that I am equally proud of <u>you</u>, a teacher. I know that you are a good teacher. I hope that you are a happy one. God bless you." The other side of the coin shows that students didn't forget him either. Corinne went by to take him to her 30th class reunion in 1985. (Corinne Wright to the author, October 29, 2015)

Mr. Oliver went to many class reunions. "Last night I attended the reunion of the 1937 Class of East Nashville High School. I could not recognize everybody." He said a high percentage of those still living were present. His former students had achieved distinctions in many fields. He often expressed his pride in their accomplishments. (Henry Oliver to the author, October 19, 1987) Ed Birthright, Class of 1956, was amazed at his remarkable memory. At a class reunion fifteen or twenty years ago, Ed told Mr. Oliver he had taught his Mother at Central High. When Ed told him his mother's name, Mr. Oliver corrected him by telling him his mother went to Jere Baxter, not Central. (Edward Birthright to the author, October 22, 2015).

Years after Mr. Oliver had passed on to his reward, his boys and girls, as he called them, still showed how much he meant to them. The former East High School had an all-class reunion September 15, 2007. Former students shared stories before that event. Joanna Henderson Blackwell said "William Henry Oliver, beloved principal at East for many years, made a point of knowing by name every student. It was said that students who misbehaved would rather get a spanking by Mr. Oliver than one of his lectures. . . If I could repeat a part of my life, it would be high school. We were so blessed to grow up in such a time and attend such a special school." (Angela Patterson, Schools section of *The Tennessean*, September 12, 2007)

The East Nashville High Alumni Association has three year reunions. They have taken bus tours through the area around their alma mater. Joanna Blackwell recalls the last time she saw Mr. Oliver before his funeral. The bus went by his home on Eastland Avenue and clad in his bathrobe, he came out the side door to speak and wave at his former students one more time. (Joanna Blackwell to the author, October 22, 2015)

What Mr. Oliver said about his years at East Nashville High contribute to a description of him as a principal. "I had about 51 years of teaching, and I enjoyed it all, but I feel my principle work was at East High School. The best thing about my years at East were my associations with the students…in my last 15 years as principal I never spanked a one, which was rather unusual at the time. But my students were good, kind and respectful. The students at East High were wonderful." In 1986, he was looking forward to seeing his former pupils at the East High Reunion. (Renee Elder Vaughn, "East High's Oliver knew his calling from the start," *The Tennessean*, November 3, 1986)

Mr. Oliver was the kind of principal who was involved in the community and knew that cooperating with the parents of his students was important. Mr. Ford, Corinne Ford Wright's Dad, owned and operated a restaurant near the high school and he was active in the East High Men's Club. The restaurant sold beer and the curb boys were told frequently not to sell it to underage students. The boys sometimes yielded to temptation when they were offered a few extra dollars. Once the police arrested Mr. Ford for selling beer to underage students as he was liable for the curb boys' actions. When he got to the police station, Mr. Oliver was there waiting for him, ready to "testify" on his behalf. Mr. Oliver said, "Mr. Ford would never willingly allow that" and that as the principal of a large high school he had to have the support of the community to keep things in line. "Mr. Ford has always done his part to help the school and to let me know when kids were skipping during the school day and the like when he was aware of it." Mr. Ford was not charged and Mr. Oliver's support was greatly appreciated. Oh if every school had such community support in the present age. (Corinne Wright to the author, October 29, 2015)

The principal of East High lived within walking distance of the school. Henry and Pauline Oliver and Pauline's mother, Mrs. McCall, lived on South 12th Street, across from 1113 Holly Street where the Kiles lived. This large house had a fenced yard to protect the Great Dane dogs Mr. Oliver raised. Mrs. Kile was a registered nurse who gave Mrs. McCall B12 shots. In appreciation for Mrs. Kile's services, the Olivers prepared a delicious dinner for this family. As a ten-year-old, Beverly indiscreetly gagged as she tasted her salad with Roquefort (blue cheese) dressing, which she had never had before. As embarrassed as she was then, she later learned to like this dressing. This was not Beverly's only memory of Mr. Oliver. When she was a ninth grader, Mrs. Walden, her civics teacher, had students to write a paper on their future vocation. Patiently, Mr. Oliver helped Beverly for many hours as she wrote about a career as a teacher. Beverly told a funny story about her Aunt Dora, called Dodo by the family, answering a phone call from Mr. Oliver. When he asked to speak to Mrs. Kile, Dodo thought the caller was "being uppity" and replied, "All right, Mr. Big Shot!" When Mr. Oliver told her who he was, she screamed, "Oh, Mr. Oliver you sounded like my brother-in-law." Of course, Mr. Oliver was the epitome of a southern gentleman and Dodo, mortified, apologized profusely; Beverly was thankful the reply was much milder than her aunt could have given. (Beverly Kile Garrett Shaw to the author, November 10, 2015)

It is now time to look at Mr. Oliver's years as principal of East Nashville High in chronological order. It is worthy to insert that he received his M.A. from Peabody College in the summer of 1939. He had done all his work for this graduate degree during summer sessions. (Henry Oliver to the author, July 5 and 25, 1974) It was not until 1987 that he was awarded an honorary Doctor of Literary Letters from Cumberland University. (Obituary in *Contact*, Summer, 1991)

December 8, 1941 conjures memories and visuals to those who were living on that date. About 850 students plus the faculty were assembled in the auditorium of East High. They listened intently to President Roosevelt call upon Congress for a declaration of war. It came and with it a new stage on which Henry Oliver would act. (Wm. Henry Oliver, Dear Joe, 1946, 57)

Like so many Americans of the era, Henry Oliver searched for his place in the World War II saga. He tried to volunteer for the chaplaincy, but was not accepted because his training was not in the proper areas. Later, he tried to enlist as a soldier; he was not accepted because of his worth as the principal of East High. Fifty-eight East Nashville High boys and one teacher were killed in that war. (Henry Oliver to the author, July 5, 1974 and June 12, 1975)

"Mr. William Henry Oliver started writing a new column in the school paper called *Dear Joe*." These words preface the eighty-eight page book which contains many of the letters Mr. Oliver wrote to the soldiers in those columns during the war years. These letters show vividly the warmth, love and concern professor Oliver had for his students. Assuredly, this facet of his personality made him the educator long remembered by former students. Mr. Oliver got a deferment for Charles Bennett so he could graduate. Charlie was scheduled to be inducted into the military in February, 1943. He graduated June 6 and went into the U.S. Army on June 13, 1943. He was in the field artillery attached to the infantry. (Charles Bennett to the author, October 22, 2015) The letters contained in Dear Joe also reveal facts about the war itself and the activities of Mr. and Mrs. Oliver during those years.

East High's principal led in a collection of scrap metal at the school. He and many others promised to bring what they could. His contribution was the barrel of the old twelve-gauge breech-loading single-barrel shotgun his father bought for John and him when he was twelve years old. Though it had personal, priceless memories, he gave it for the common good. After giving this piece with such sentimental value on October 30, 1942, he went to the train station to bid his brother, John, Godspeed as he left for naval training in Norfolk, Virginia. (Dear Joe, 6, 13)

> We firmly believe that the best men are the best soldiers . . . . You cannot be as good a soldier if you drink . . . . There are four names who lead our foes. Hitler, Tojo, and Mussolini are three. The other is John Barleycorn. All are deadly enemies of the ideals for which you fight. And of these four, Barleycorn has probably . . . filled more graves than all the other three combined . . . . He is a demon . . . . Beware of him! (Dear Joe, 21)

Was this a speech by some local chairman of the Temperance Committee or a sermon from a fundamental pulpit? No. It was the urgency of a high school principal conveyed to those young men he tried to educate—intellectually, physically, spiritually and morally. One cannot help but think how different education is in today's average high school!

During the week of February 22-27 more than 7,000 people registered at East High for ration book Number Two. ". . . The people . . . were the nicest, finest, most cooperative large cross-section of the human race that I have ever seen . . . I look at my girls and my boys . . . I watch them . . . laugh and sing and play together. And I wish fervently that I could keep them as happy as they are now." (Dear Joe, 21) These are examples of Henry Oliver's optimistic outlook on life and his heartfelt concern for his students.

Mr. Oliver was in a soldier's tent in November of 1943 with his ROTC boys encamped at Percy Warner Park. He identified with his students although it may have been before the days when educators proclaimed from their ivory halls of learning that to teach, one must be identified with one's students. But what was sleeping in a tent for one night compared to the sacrifices of those enlisted? ". . . I was ashamed of myself and of many of my fellows who sacrifice so little while you and your buddies sacrifice so much."

The principal of East High "preached a sermon" entitled "Christmas, 1943-The Christian Way." There were three points in the outline, based upon the three principles of the Christian way of life. First, God is the loving Father of all mankind. Second, the golden rule's purpose is to guide men in their dealings with others. Third, the human soul is immortal. Mr. Oliver intended this to comfort the fellows who had watched their buddies die. "And may this be the last ne that you must spend away from home." (Dear Joe, 34-39)

His letter of May 15, 1944 showed the humility and depth of unselfishness that Mr. Oliver possessed.

> If only I could feel that I am helping you, I should not feel so tired and useless at the close of the day. What have I done today? I've seen a score of teachers and hundreds of students. With many of them I've exchanged greetings and smiles. Some I've talked with. Some I've reprimanded. Some I've praised. Are they any better for our association? Am I? I was not working for my benefit. Or was I? After all, why do I spend my time trying to get the loafer to study, the quitter to stick. . .boys and girls to build character and get an education? The public pays me well . . . I wonder whether I am worth the pay. To me every individual seems precious; and the worst scalawag worth saving . . .What can man do for youth? Youth who thinks that he himself knows everything and that he is quite capable of making his own decisions-all decisions? . . . Friends have helped me all my life, not because I could offer them anything, but because I needed help. (Dear Joe, 47)

He in turn was striving to do the same for others. It did not matter that it took hard work to do that. "We need not ask for lighter labor but for greater strength."

"Not even war has stopped the music of young America." That's what Henry Oliver said at the end of the annual marching contest for Middle Tennessee high school bands held in Keyes Stadium at East High on April 21, 1944.

About 700 students from twelve schools composed one giant band to render a magnificent rendition of "The Star Spangled Banner."

Overall, the youth at East High had basically the same educational opportunities as they had before the war. Few classes failed to meet due to lack of teachers, and there was no scarcity of the essential materials. Extracurricular and inter-school activities were not curtailed. "We still have our clubs, our athletics, our dramatics, our chorus, our school paper, our lunch room." There was more emotional stress than in normal times. Home life had been disrupted with fathers and mothers off to war and mothers working in defense plants and elsewhere. (Dear Joe, 48, 55-56)

There were East High graduates that contributed to the war effort although they were not in the military. At a plant in Nashville, John Steinhauer, 1944 graduate, built B-38 fighter planes for the U.S. Army Air Force as it was called then. About a hundred B-38s were built at the plant. On an interesting note, John swam and ate with Franklin Delano Roosevelt in Warm Springs, Georgia. (John Steinhauer to the author, October 22, 2015)

The school day was over for April 12, 1945 and many were gathered in the stadium for a baseball game between East High and Montgomery Bell Academy. Over the radio came the startling news that Franklin D. Roosevelt had died. The game was stopped momentarily for prayer. The next morning the student body gathered in the auditorium for songs, Bible reading and prayer in honor of the deceased President. A former student on the war front wrote his former principal that he was proud just to have lived in the same generation with so great an American as

President Roosevelt. Such sentiments were shared by many young Americans of that era.

President Harry S. Truman made the formal announcement on May 11, 1945 that the war in Europe was over because the German armies had surrendered unconditionally. The few teachers and students already at East High that morning went to the auditorium for Bible reading and prayer. They then went home as the day was proclaimed as a holiday. Many Nashville churches had services of thanksgiving. Henry Oliver attended one at St. Ann's Episcopal Church. (Dear Joe, 67-69)

In 1983, Mr. Oliver received the prestigious Leon Gilbert Memorial Award from the American Legion Post 5. One facet of his award nomination by Percy C. Miller, Hugh R. Mott and Florence V. Slavin said:

> Mr. Oliver looked with pride as several of the teachers of East High and over eighteen hundred students and former students served in the Armed Forces during World War II. He sorrowfully saw one teacher and fifty-eight of his boys fail to survive this war. Mr. Oliver started a column in the school paper during WWII called "Dear Joe" in which he wrote letters to those in the armed services. It is impossible to assess how valuable these letters were to the hundreds of G.I.s who hungered for any news from home. Many of these letters expressed the warmth, love, concern and respect Mr. Oliver had for his students. These feelings were mutual since all who knew Mr. William Henry Oliver loved and respected him. ("Former East High Principal Oliver Dies," *Nashville Banner*, May 16, 1991)

Mr. Oliver was a part of a variety of activities on Thanksgiving Day of 1945. He gave the devotion at a breakfast at the First Church of the Nazarene and sang in the choir at St. Ann's at the ten o'clock Holy Communion service. He felt both thankfulness and unworthiness. That afternoon, he and Mrs. Oliver attended the all-star football game at Vanderbilt University in Dudley Stadium. That evening they went to the Ryman Auditorium to hear the Russian Cossacks sing. The music was performed magnificently and with feeling. This day showed the broad interests of Henry Oliver and his ability to thoroughly enjoy them all.

> Some who had not graduated have re-entered school at East, others at Hume-Fogg Tech . . . Many . . . who had graduated are now in college, some have gone back to their old jobs, others are . . . taking a . . . much-needed rest. Comparatively few have been badly crippled by injuries received in service. Some, however have; and some—too many—are still in military hospitals . . .When you get home, Joe, you must get the past off your mind . . . past is past. Only in the future is there hope . . . You will find America, though full of problems, still a land of opportunity. (Dear Joe, 82, 87-88)

With this optimistic advice for the resumption of peace time living, William Henry Oliver closed his letters to "*Dear Joe.*"

And what were the years after the war like? What progress was made at East Nashville High School? As the principal of East High, Mr. Oliver was very dedicated to his task. A history of the school will in a very real sense be a history of those years of his life. "We love you, for what you are making of us . . . . You have done it by being yourself. Perhaps, that is what being a friend means, after all." That's the way the staff of the 1946 *Grey Eagle*, East High's annual, expressed their thoughts about William Henry Oliver. Several items of interest were in the "Class History" in the same annual. Teen-Town, which proved to be of great recreational value to the school and community, was organized during the 1943-1944 term by the Young Women's Christian Association. (Nancy Gossage, editor, *Grey Eagle*, 1946) East High had asked for Teen-Town which offered good, wholesome fun for the young people, meeting in the basement of the library. The 1944-1945 term brought several new organizations to East High. One was a religious program, "Going Our Way." The School Spirit Club and the Vocal Ensemble were also added. The Ensemble was one of the best vocal groups in the city. Baseball was reintroduced in the spring of 1945 to the delight of East High's fans. The 1945-1946 term saw the return of three faculty members who had served in the Armed Forces. W. Carman (Willie) Campbell, Harwood Tilton and Watson Magee were welcomed back by Principal Oliver, the faculty and students. Dr. John L. Hill, editorial secretary of the Southern Baptist Sunday School Board, gave a speech. Coupled with music by the Ensemble and a talk by George Cate, the Alumni Association's President, this was a fitting memorial to the boys who had given their last full measure of devotion during the war. (Nancy Gossage, editor, *Grey Eagle*, 1946.) Mr. Oliver had "Going Our Way" used in homerooms. He played a large part in organizing the material. A book of programs, highly devotional in nature, was prepared. Mr. Oliver's indelible mark was made when a number of poems were included. This book was made available to all the city schools. (Henry Oliver to the author, June 18, 1975)

Elizabeth B. Browning's Sonnet XLIII is usually thought of in connection with romantic lovers. Yet, it was deemed an appropriate selection for Mr. Oliver by the students of the Class of 1947. Under his picture in the annual we find "How do we love thee? Let us count the ways . . . ." During the 1946-1947 term, the *Eagle* staff sponsored the publication of Dear Joe, a compilation of Mr. Oliver's letters written to service men for the school newspaper. That same year the Dramatic Guild held its first musical in the school's history, "A Date with Judy." (Betty Anne Cavender, editor, *Grey Eagle*, 1947)

The history of the Class of 1948 shows changes and progress at East High. In their sophomore year (1945-1946), ROTC was made compulsory for all sophomore boys with two units required for graduation. The Alumni Association had erected a clock on top of the school as a memorial to the boys who lost their lives in the war. By the fall of 1947 the Hunting and Fishing Club and the Camera Club had been organized. The boys division of the Boy-Girl Friendship Club came into existence, and the joint groups held forums on boy-girl relations. Nashville schools organized bowling teams, and East was well represented among the city's teams. (Peggy Fuson, editor, *Grey Eagle*, 1948)

According to Peggy Fuson Hoyal, Mr. Oliver was one of a kind. Not only was he the principal but he served as guidance counselor, psychologist and friend. Peggy went to him in tears when Buddy broke a date for the 1947 Junior-Senior only three days before the big event. Mr. Oliver listened and cared that this upset his student. He gave her a note to be excused from English class, stating that she was in his office. Peggy said he was never too busy to listen and to help figure out solutions to what students thought were big dilemmas. Mr. Oliver provided transportation for the cheerleaders to away football games in his big Olds. Peggy also recalled how he coordinated efforts of the Civinettes and Civitans when they sold papers on Palm Sunday to benefit crippled children. (Peggy Fuson Hoyal to the author, September 26, 2015)

The Class of 1949 expressed their gratitude for one who had planned for, prayed for, inspired, and trusted in them. That one had strength and beauty of character along with being the ideal of Christian living. "His life of purity and virtue has woven itself into the heart of every East High Student." That one, of course, was William Henry Oliver. In the fall of 1946, the Student Council officers were inaugurated at East High. The Class of 1949 sat as "silly sophomores" listening as Mr. Oliver sang "My Task" with such feeling and sincerity that they were not to forget it. During the 1946-1947 term, East was represented for the first time at the Columbia Scholastic Press Association's annual convention held at Columbia University in New York City. The Allied Youth Club was organized in May of 1949 and the Fishing Club began in the same year. The 1949 annual had a snapshot of "Hank the Harmonica Player;" however, "Hank" wasn't a student; it was Mr. Oliver playing that instrument which he had played for years. (Mary Ann Stevens, editor, *Grey Eagle*, 1949) According to Mr. Oliver, the Allied Youth Club was an anti-alcohol club. Its purpose was to inform young people as to the evils of beverage alcohol and to protect them from its use.

Mr. Oliver received a Master's in Education in 1949 from Peabody College with a major in Educational Administration. The work he did was equivalent to an Education Specialist degree today. All of the work was done in summer sessions or on a part time basis during other sessions. (Henry Oliver to the author, June 18, 1975)

The Class of 1950 recalled the new constitution for school government that was instituted in the 1947-1948 school term. Highlights from the 1948-1949 term included the girls' basketball team winning the Eighth District Championship. Also, the Chorus performed Handel's "Hallelujah Chorus" for the first time, a rather unique accomplishment for any high school group. The school's paper, *The Eagle*, rated second in the *Nashville Banner's* Mid-State Newspaper Contest. East's National Forensic League won first and second place in All-State Competition. The Inner-City Student Council was founded during the 1949-1950 term with the East Nashville Council playing a major role. The "Last Will and Testament" from the Class of 1950 left Mr. Oliver with a few more gray hairs, for which they apologized. They thanked him for his patience, kindness and unforgettable love. (Evelyn Louis Steven, editor, *Grey Eagle*, 1950)

The Class of 1951 classified Mr. Oliver as their beloved principal and the beacon light of their hearts. "May we, in the faithful living of our lives, give back to him some part of that which he has given to us in inspiration, devotion, and guidance." That class distributed fifty-two Christmas baskets in 1948 to needy families. In September, 1949, new fluorescent lights, file cabinets, modern chromium kitchen appliances for home economics, and an electric scoreboard for the football field were installed. The Journalism Club of

1950-1951 was awarded one of the highest honors given to a high school paper, a first from the Columbia Scholastic Press Association. The Drivers Training course was added in the spring of 1950. The Student Council of 1950-1951 had sidewalks repaired, the tennis courts finished, purchased a new curtain for the stage, organized a pep club, and began work on a school handbook. (Mindel Gardenshire and Elizabeth McKnight, editors, *Grey Eagle*, 1951)

    As a member of the Class of 1952, Beverly Kile Garrett Shaw recalled one of the worst blizzards in the history of Nashville. In February, 1951, there was no school for two days, the only time in her ten years in Nashville Public Schools that she recalled school being closed for bad weather. Beverly was sweeping the front walk and so was her neighbor, Mr. Oliver. A boy in her class came trudging up the street with his eyes almost closed. She asked him where he was going in all the snow. He mumbled, "To school." He didn't believe her when she said school was closed. Beverly said, "Well, there is our principal, Mr. Oliver, sweeping his sidewalk. Will you believe him?" He mumbled something about going home, turned and trudged back toward his house. A few weeks before her graduation in 1952, Mr. Oliver called Beverly into his office. She was an honor student who didn't cause trouble; so she was apprehensive. Mr. Oliver told her how proud he was of all she had accomplished at East and appreciated how she never misbehaved in all the years he had known her. Beverly was overwhelmed and completely surprised. Not only did he share this with her but he planned to tell her parents. "I was very blessed to have a neighbor and principal like Mr. Oliver and to this day I know I learned many worthwhile intangibles from him . . . mostly from his shining example as a Christian gentleman." (Beverly Kile Garrett Shaw to the author, November 10, 2015)

The 1953 *Grey Eagle* was dedicated to Mr. Oliver for his Christian leadership, patience, understanding, and willingness to help. The yearbook had a new section as the sophomores and juniors were included for the first time. The Class History mentioned the Evaluation by the Southern Association for Accreditation in 1951-1952 which made the school fully accredited for nine more years. The Association required a self-study every ten years after which this accreditation was granted. (Katharine Bryan, editor, *Grey Eagle*, 1953)

The 1954 *Grey Eagle* was also dedicated to the principal. This time it was for his individual companionship with "his children" and wholeheartedly supporting all their endeavors and for his constant guidance. The "Last Will and Testament" of the Class of 1954 left their gratitude to Mr. Oliver for just being a "regular guy." Their Class History told of the Tennessee Association of Student Councils meeting at East High during the 1951-1952 term. Students kept the delegates in their homes. (Ida Jo Simpson, editor, *Grey Eagle*, 1954)

A fire in the lunchroom during the junior year of the Class of 1955 caused damage only to kitchen equipment. The school had its first Career Day the same year. There are pictures of the rifle, track, golf and tennis teams in the 1955 yearbook. For the first time, there was a picture of "Miss East High." (Barbara Davis, editor, *Grey Eagle*, 1955) Jewell (Spencer) Painter, member of the Class of 1955, told about going to Mr. Oliver with a request to leave school early because her baby brother was being born sixteen years after her birth. Mr. Oliver's response was, "Why did you even come to school today?" This was just the kind of guy he was. (Jewell Painter to the author, October 22, 2015) Corrine Ford Wright, another member of this class, shared another story. She told of her Shorthand II class. Mr. Oliver would ask Mrs. McGowan, the teacher, to send someone to take letters he dictated. The girls were scared that they wouldn't be fast enough and wouldn't translate correctly or be able to type well enough to suit him. Corinne's turn came; he kindly asked her to sit down and began his dictation - so slowly that she thought he would NEVER get through. Due to his thoughtfulness, none of the girls had any problems typing his letters.

Seniors in the 1950s were required to write an essay in English classes for a contest. They were free to select the subject for the essay. Corinne was engaged in many extra-curricular activities and wasn't very interested in putting much time into the assignment. She called her essay "What I Will Remember about High School Days at East." Shortly afterwards, Mr. Oliver summoned her to his office. Since she wasn't in any trouble, she was puzzled. He really liked the essay, but it had not won the contest. She wrote about things he hoped many students would remember about their high school days. Some of those things were wonderful extra-curricular activities, choral concerts, school pride, friendships, Teen Town and the Noel Ball Show. Judging by the many stories his former students have shared, they certainly did! Mr. Oliver knew that a good high school and developing good citizens involved much more than just classes and books. Corinne, who had a long career as a high school teacher, concluded with, "I know my classmates and I grew up in a truly special time called the 50's, had many good teachers, a well-rounded education for the times and a great neighborhood school called East High, home of the soaring grey eagles. I wish every kid in America today could have such warm, good memories."

Mr. Oliver's involvement with students did not end when they graduated. Mr. Oliver secured for Corinne her first summer job after high school at Washington Manufacturing Company where she made eighty-nine cents an hour. She worked in the Purchasing Department, which was headed by Mr. Oliver's lovely wife, Pauline. She was always gracious to Corinne, vivacious and sweet, yet very professional. Years later, Corinne would have loved to see her; she was saddened when Mr. Oliver told her that she wouldn't recognize her. After her death, Corinne wrote Mr. Oliver and told him how she remembered his wife when she worked for her. That letter meant a lot to Mr. Oliver. (Corinne Wright to the author, October 29, 2015)

The Beta Club at East Nashville High was organized in 1955-1956; however, East already had the National Honor Society. The bowling team is pictured for the first time. The Class of 1956 left Mr. Oliver an abundant supply of patience as they had used all of his last supply. (Marjorie Haden, editor, *Grey Eagle*, 1956)

The 1957 *Grey Eagle* staff called Mr. Oliver "the guiding hand, the kindly sympathizer." Their Class History says the 1954-1955 football team became the first Nashville Interscholastic League team to go by plane to another city. Teen Town was permanently established at East. The Civinette and Civitan Club float won first prize in the Fire Prevention Parade during the 1956-1957 term. The Male Chorus was chosen to sing for the Southern Music Educators Conference in Miami Beach, Florida in the spring, which was quite an honor. The Art and Science Clubs and the Quill and Scroll were added during the year. (Anita Farrar, editor, *Grey Eagle*, 1957)

Joanna Henderson Blackwell, member of the Class of 1959, was in the eighth grade at East Nashville Junior High when the Junior High band began marching with the Senior High band. She was a majorette from 8th through 12th grades. The bands practiced on the Keyes Stadium football field. One day, as she was returning to East Junior after practice, Joanna encountered the big man himself, Mr. Oliver. He introduced himself, as if she didn't know who he was, and began to engage in conversation. He asked about her interests and goals and how she liked school. When Joanna started to high school, Mr. Oliver remembered their meeting, as well as her name. This is a memory Joanna has never forgotten. Mr. Oliver was a kind man, a mentor to many and now he is a legend to all who knew him. (Joanna Henderson Blackwell to the author, September 20, 2015)

"And lo, it was in the Spring of the year that the multitude was told by our beloved William H. Oliver, that he had been promoted and there were many tears spread throughout the kingdom and many grieved over the loss of our great leader." The 1958 *Grey Eagle* was dedicated to him as past principal. He had been more than a principal or even a close personal friend. He was more like a father to many. One always came from his office strengthened and encouraged. Mere words did not express the deep feeling or repay the debt of gratitude. (Helen Gibson, editor, *Grey Eagle*, 1958)

The feeling of his being like a father still persisted in 1975 as he received Father's Day cards from former students. Among these were Barbara Morgan, Geraldine Heidbreder and Betty Grice Bibb. (Henry Oliver to the author, June 18, 1975) Gratitude continued to be expressed by his former students from East High. "Just a note to let you know how much your influence . . . has meant to me . . . . Almost daily I see cases of young men with no guidance who are going down the wrong path and think that 'There but for the grace of God and Mr. Oliver go I.'"(Dickie Fuqua to Henry Oliver, June 10, 1975, Oliver Collection.) This fellow graduated in 1952 after Mr. Oliver had patiently disciplined him many times and wondered what he would ever amount to. In 1975 he was the President-Treasurer of the Tennessee Adjustment Service. Yes, that is the joy of teaching!

Some of Mr. Oliver's students have been mentioned by name but as this section comes to a close, a review of students reveals other names that the reader may find of interest. When he was at Hume-Fogg, Dinah Shore was a student there. She was called "Fanny Rose" back then and auditioned for a talent show. "She sang *Paradise* and she had a sweet, soft contralto. . . Some of the members of the committee didn't think she was good enough. I stood up for her and I still like to hear her. Fanny Rose is one of my favorite girls." After this comment, Mr. Oliver sang a few bars of *Paradise*. Actor Frank Sutton who played Sgt. Carter on the Gomer Pyle show was a student at East High during Mr. Oliver's years there. Joe Casey, Nashville's Chief of Police in the 1980s, wasn't his student but he married one of his girls. The list of his former students also included U.S. Representative Bill Bonner, Nashville businessmen Owen Howell, Tommy Parker and Bobby Garrison. (Jennifer Plant, "W.H. Oliver recalls his full life as an educator" *Nashville Banner*, September 3, 1983)

What did Mr. Oliver do during the summers of the time period covered in this chapter? A variety of things! To omit these would be like leaving out pieces of a puzzle. One summer he worked for the Washington Manufacturing Company doing manual labor in the shirt department where he filled orders and did several other things for an hourly wage of one dollar. For a number of summers he taught in the Peabody Demonstration School, an elementary and secondary school where they experimented with a variety of new teaching methods. Mr. Oliver taught English to grades ten through twelve as well as "Child Development and Guidance" one summer. In 1931, he and other educators organized a private summer school and were allowed to use the city's books and buildings. The educators charged tuition and it was divided among those who taught. The Board of Education later took over the summer school program; Mr. Oliver no longer worked in summer school.

Mr. Oliver also served on the Accreditation Board of the Southern Association of Secondary Schools and Colleges as one of the three members from Tennessee. He served on the committee that considered applications for membership from junior colleges and special schools. Committee members studied the reports and records sent by these schools and made recommendations to the board as to whether or not accreditation was recommended. Each committee member had six to ten schools to review. Mr. Oliver recalled passing on Mt. Olive College in North Carolina and a small school in Lebanon, Tennessee. He also considered schools in Georgia, Alabama and Louisiana. He served as chairman of three evaluation committees at schools in his area which work was not a part of being on the board. Twice he was the chairman at David Lipscomb and once at

St. Bernard's, both private, church-related schools. (Henry Oliver to the author, June 12 and 18, 1975)

During the years from 1930-1957, Henry Oliver filled many speaking engagements. He spoke to a variety of audiences with various interests. The notes from his speeches and sermons are most interesting. Some notes were used on twelve or fifteen different occasions, some used as long as fifty years after he made the notes. General observation of his notes showed his wide span of interests, his broad knowledge gained from reading in many fields, and his love of poetry.

A theme William Henry Oliver often used was "God's Way or Mine?" Sometimes it had another title and was something other than a sermon. The central thought was always "God's way is wise; man's is foolish." He used these thoughts at various functions and in many churches. He spoke on this topic at the Reformatory School in Bordeaux. (Henry Oliver, October 14, 1934, Oliver Collection)

On at least two occasions and those over twenty years apart, he spoke on "Take a Lead and Keep It." The first time he used this theme was in 1935 at the Lockeland Church's Basketball Banquet. Then in 1959 he used it for the North Nashville High School Honor Society. He compared life to a game to be played with youth in the first inning. The admonition was "Take a Lead and Keep It" with the added thought of "Don't go out on fouls." That last topic was used at Gallatin Road Baptist Church in 1955 when East Nashville High's principal spoke at their Basketball Banquet. He answered two questions. 1) What constitutes a foul? 2) What causes a foul? He went on to discuss the results. Yes, life is like a game, but it has no seasons; it is played year round. Life is not divided into eight minute quarters, but it is played for life. Mr. Oliver closed by asking "What will spectators say at the close of the game?" (Henry Oliver, April, 1935, April 25, 1955 and December 5, 1957, Oliver Collection)

Easter signifies new life through redemption of Jesus Christ to all Christians. It holds the blessed hope that the dead in Christ shall live again. Henry Oliver proclaimed these thoughts in 1935 at the Tennessee State Training School (Reformatory for Boys) on Hydes Ferry Pike. His remarks were titled "The Meaning of Easter to You." (Henry Oliver, April 14, 1935, Oliver Collection)

Mr. Oliver selected "Is the Young Man Absalom Safe?" as his topic at least twice. In 1946, he spoke to the Parent Teacher Association's Annual Father's Night at Bailey Junior High in Nashville. This speech was based on the father, David, and his son, Absalom. David loved Absalom, but he neglected part of his training. He emphasized the importance of teaching sons how to live. On Father's Day, 1974, Brother Oliver used these thoughts again at East Nashville Free Will Baptist Church. (Henry Oliver, November 14, 1946 and June 14, 1974, Oliver Collection)

Professor Oliver spoke to fathers again on the Parent Teacher Association's Father's Night at Glenn School in Nashville. He talked of his own father who had been a living example to him, who gave him the ideals by which he lived every day. He also used some of these thoughts on another Father's Day when he spoke at Madison Church of God. (Henry Oliver, February 25, 1949 and Father's Day, 1963, Oliver Collection)

"Victorious Living" wove its way into addresses Henry Oliver gave. Man was not made for slavery. It is glorious to feel victorious, but where lies the difference? It is in the attitude of the mind and heart—in faith. This address was delivered at a Junior-Senior Banquet at Free Will Baptist Bible College. (Henry Oliver, 1950, Oliver Collection)

The Tennessee Teachers Association of Business Colleges held workshops at the James Robertson Hotel in 1951. Henry Oliver addressed those present on "What a High School Principal Expects of a Business College." He listed good courses, good equipment and teachers and some supervision of conduct. (Henry Oliver, May 12, 1951, Oliver Collection)

Professor Oliver also spoke in Belmont College's chapel. He gave his ideas on choosing as he mentioned right choices that need to be made during the college years. He challenged his listeners to make their college years a time of strengthening religious faith. (Henry Oliver, September 14, 1951, Oliver Collection)

The youth group of the First Lutheran Church were the Luther Leaguers. At their banquet in 1952, Mr. Oliver admonished the Luther Leaguers to beware of bad company. He further told them not to be a smart Alek or a quitter. Can one be a Christian and still be one of the crowd? If not, one should get out of the crowd. The "should" needed to have a purpose in life and to take time to prepare for life. (Henry Oliver, May 23, 1952, Oliver Collection)

In 1953, Henry Oliver, the public educator, was the keynote speaker for David Lipscomb High School's commencement. He plainly said youth were not going to the dogs. Any youth who did were often dragged there by their elders. All generations have prodigal sons, but there have always been great youngsters, too. He admonished youth to live independently, acknowledging one Master—God Himself. (Henry Oliver, May 28, 1953, Oliver Collection)

Mr. Oliver, the guest speaker, arose and began to speak at Trevecca College's Junior-Senior Banquet in 1954. He elaborated on frontiers, keeping in mind the theme, "Pioneering New Frontiers." There were various kinds of frontiers; he used Columbus, the Apostle Paul, Lindberg, and Edison as examples. He gave pointers for what was needed for a new frontier. "Sail On, Sail On!" was an appropriate poem, rendered as only William Henry Oliver could. (Henry Oliver, May 22, 1954, Oliver Collection)

Mr. Oliver spoke on "More Abundant Living in a Democracy" twice in 1955. First, he addressed the Inter-High Student Council at Donelson High; second, he spoke at a service honoring the graduating seniors at the First Church of the Nazarene. "It lies within each individual with God's help, to make glorious and rich and beautiful and abundant his or her own life. . . ." (Henry Oliver, May 2, 1955 and May 22, 1955, Oliver Collection)

In 1956, Mr. Oliver spoke at the Basketball Banquet at Belmont College where he presented two main ideas. 1) You are fortunate. 2) You are important. "Tomorrow awaits you; humanity needs you; God is counting on you. Get in there and fight. You can win . . . ." (Henry Oliver, March 11, 1956, Oliver Collection)

Free Will Baptist Bible College's graduates were privileged to listen to Henry Oliver in 1957. He took the title of "The Old Rail Fence" from a story in his boyhood. He lived on a very steep hill near Indian Mound; often he had to carry water from the valley below. He usually paused to rest by an old rail fence. He compared graduation to his climbing the hill and pausing to rest. The graduates had come up a long hill; it was appropriate to pause for rest. In that pause, Mr. Oliver sketched part of the climb in the past and then reminded them that the rest of the hill remained to be climbed. (Henry Oliver, May 30, 1957, Oliver Collection) "Strange to say, when I went to Free Will Baptist Bible College as a teacher five years ago, I discovered that some of the folk still remembered 'The Old Rail Fence.'" (Henry Oliver to the author, June 18, 1975) Perhaps, the last statement shows how the way Mr. Oliver's words lingered in the minds of his hearers down through the years.

What better topic for Gideons than "You and Your Bible." He used those notes again at East Nashville Free Will Baptist Church at the "Kick-Off" Sunday for that church's golden anniversary. Since Bro. Oliver was the first pastor, he was asked to bring the message. The thoughts were mainly on how to study the Bible and the results of studying and putting into practice the Word of God. (Henry Oliver, July 3, 1957 and September 14, 1973, Oliver Collection)

The Nashville Boys Club assembled at Montgomery Bell State Park in 1957 where Mr. Oliver spoke about courage. He advised them to have the courage to take correction with the right spirit, to do right, and to be reverent toward God. (Henry Oliver, July 7, 1957, Oliver Collection)

This is a very slim sampling of the speeches Mr. Oliver gave during these years. Glancing through his notes, one can see that he spoke before these clubs: Kiwanis, Civitans, Optimists, Exchange, Scottish Rite and men's clubs. Other groups included Young Men's Christian Association (YMCA) and National Sorority of Phi Delta Kappa, Alpha Beta Chapter. Although he was a Free Will Baptist minister, Rev. Oliver spoke to many denominational groups. Other than the ones already mentioned, he spoke in these churches: Cumberland Presbyterian, Christian, Methodist, Presbyterian, Episcopal and African-American. David Lipscomb University is affiliated with the Church of Christ and Trevecca College is affiliated with the Nazarene Church. Of course, he spoke to numerous branches of Baptist churches. William Henry Oliver was not reduced to the narrow bounds of any group whether religious or otherwise.

A glimpse back over the time spanned in this chapter shows how impossible it was to entirely cover the activities of these years. Picture a man going to the various functions of a big city high school in addition to fulfilling all the duties of the principal of that school. Then in his "spare time," imagine him preaching almost every weekend in a church within a seventy-five mile radius of Nashville. Intersperse addresses given to various groups, attendance at local functions of interest, and the few activities you could categorize as a part of his personal life. Maybe, just maybe, that gives an accurate image of William Henry Oliver's life from 1930 through 1957.

The Olivers' home at 201 South 12th St.

The Olivers' home at 1500 Eastland Ave.

East Nashville High School
The clock, 59" in diameter, over the entrance to the building is dedicated to the 58 East High graduates who lost their lives in World War II.
Photos of the houses and the school from Corinne Wright

This photo of Mr. Oliver is from the 1951 *Eagle*. He was "the beacon-light of our hearts." "May we, in the faithful living of our lives, give back to him some part of that which he has given to us in inspiration, devotion, and guidance."
The 1953 *Eagle* was dedicated to him with the following words.

Dr. Dale E. Young
Founded Upon A Rock

"We, the Senior class, dedicate this . . .yearbook . . . to our principal; for his Christian leadership, which has become a beacon guiding our lives; for his unfailing willingness to aid us in each minute problem; and his patience and understanding of each individual. These characteristics have made our years at East more profitable."

Photo provided by Joanna Blackwell

The exact date of this photo is unknown but it was during Mr. Oliver's years at East Nashville High.

This picture of Mrs. Oliver must have been made at the same time as the one of Mr. Oliver. These pictures of the Olivers hang in the Fellowship Hall at Dunbar's Chapel FWB Church. Henry Oliver gave them to the church several years before his death.
    Pictures provided by Francis (Turner) Webb

Dr. Dale E. Young | 117
Founded Upon A Rock

Mr. Oliver speaks at the 40th reunion of the Class of 1948. The man on the left is Jim Hoyal and on the right is Billy Harrell who drove Mr. Oliver whenever he was needed.
**Photo from Peggy F. Hoyal.
Both she and Jim graduated in 1948.**

William Henry Oliver in his office at

East Nashville High School

Photo provided by Joanna Blackwell

Chapter 5

SEVEN YEARS AT THE HELM

(1957-1964)

William Henry Oliver had a wide range of experience to his credit by 1957. A respected educator with high standards, he expended a great deal of personal concern for individual students as well as teachers and other fellow workers. His experience qualified him well for the vacancy created when W.A. Bass stepped down from the position of Superintendent of Nashville City Schools. Little did Mr. Oliver realize that he would be the last man to fill that post due to the creation of a Metropolitan Government from the merging of the city and county governments. He would be at the helm when desegregation came to this Southern city. He would also work diligently toward an effective merger between the Davidson County and Nashville City Schools.

"Mrs. Bland moved that the Board elect Mr. William Henry Oliver as Assistant Superintendent effective July 1,

1957 through December 31, 1957 at an annual salary of $9,000 per year." This motion passed and the Board proceeded to elect him as Superintendent effective January 1, 1958 for one year at a salary to be negotiated. (Minutes of Board of Education, City of Nashville, May 21, 1957. Hereafter, referred to as Minutes) The salary agreed upon was $12,000 a year. The public announcement of his appointment came on his twenty-ninth anniversary, May 22, 1957. This launched Mr. Oliver's seven year journey at the head of a large city school system. In his characteristic manner, he entered into this new job seeking God's help. After thanking the Board for placing their confidence in him, he said the Lord being his Helper, he would do his utmost to justify their confidence. (Minutes, June 12, 1957)

During his years as superintendent, Henry Oliver experienced the loss of two family members. In May, 1960, his dear Mother Frances Lavonia Hembree Oliver passed away at the home of his sister, Mrs. Eddis Stanley. She was survived by fourteen grandchildren and two great-grandchildren. Her funeral was at East Nashville Free Will Baptist Church, conducted by Rev. J.L. Welch, assisted by Rev. Charles Thigpen and Rev. Dale Burden. Mrs. Oliver was interred beside her late husband, J.H. Oliver, in Hayes Cemetery in Stewart County. In November of the same year, Ruby Oliver, Henry's sister, left this earthly life. Her funeral was also at the East Nashville Church and was conducted by the pastor at that time, Rev. Dale Burden. Her body was laid to rest back in Stewart County in the Hayes Cemetery. (Obituaries, 1960)

Many items of significance crossed the Superintendent's desk during the next seven years. It was difficult to sift through the events to glean those that would be included here. Two matters that have had the most far-reaching effects were those pertaining to desegregation and the merging that formed what is known as Metro. First, there is a section on desegregation. Second, there is an overview of the activities from 1957 to 1964. Third, there is a brief summary of the work that paved the way for the Metropolitan Board of Education.

In 1964, the Supreme Court passed down its decision that was to bring sweeping reforms in the area of desegregation. Before the fall of 1957, the Nashville Board of Education was challenged as to its position on the issue. A request for an injunction against the Board was made for refusing admission of African-American students to white schools and vice versa. Before a course of action was determined, the Board assured the judge that it was planning to submit a plan for desegregation. The court did not issue the injunction. The first grade was integrated that fall and the Board was required to submit a plan for all grades before December 31, 1957.

The school term began on September 9, 1957. As a result of organized efforts, disorder was prevalent at all the white schools where African-American students enrolled. People congregated on school grounds and molested African-Americans trying to enter and solicited whites to withdraw from the school. Such disorder continued all day and into the night. That night one inflammatory meeting was held in at least one school and in one public square where agitators attempted to arouse listeners to prevent the court order from being enforced. The Hattie Cotton Elementary School on West Greenwood Avenue was badly damaged by a dynamite blast at 12:30 a.m. on September 10. Disorder continued throughout the next day and arrests were made.

The Police Department was out in force to protect lives and property and to maintain law and order. The Board viewed all these actions as defiance of the U.S. District Court at Nashville and of the law of the land. They requested the U.S. Attorney to investigate and determine who was responsible and to take prompt injunctive action or whatever was necessary to restrain such future action. Mr. Oliver and Mayor Ben West spent a lot of time in the U.S. Attorney General's office in an effort to begin measures to restore peace and order. Federal Judge William E. Miller issued an order restraining twelve segregationists from interfering with desegregation in Nashville. This was the first step toward securing a permanent injunction. (Minutes, September 10 and 12, 1957) These were the beginnings of desegregation in Nashville. No, there was not perfect order. However, the situations were handled wisely. Dealing with such incidents reflected Mr. Oliver's fairness to all. Remember, this is the man who as a child thought it unfair that his Cherokee friend could not attend school with him.

The Instruction Committee presented its plan for desegregation to the Board on December 4, 1957. "No compulsory integration or segregation shall be required in any grade of the Nashville Public School System." The plan consisted of two elements. 1) Desegregation of one grade at a time was to take place. The first grade was desegregated in 1957, the second grade to be desegregated in 1958, and so on. 2) Any parent who had a child in a school or a class in which the majority of the students were of another race could request a transfer to another school. Many school systems in other states followed this plan. The second element would be struck down by the court later. Parents were required to give reasons other than racial for a transfer. They then gave "acceptable" reasons although race may have been a major one. Mr. Oliver personally decided on every transfer requested. (Henry Oliver to the author, June 18, 1975) Three groups of schools with equal standards, opportunities, and facilities were to be provided. These were schools for African-Americans whose parents preferred that their children be educated with members of their own race exclusively; schools for white students whose parents preferred the same; integrated schools for those whose parents preferred schools available to those of both races. The attorneys for Nashville City Schools were Edwin Hunt and Reber Boult. At a hearing on April 14, 1958, the District Court approved the plans as set forth. (Minutes, December 4, 1957 and April 9, 1958)

On March 5, 1959, Mr. Oliver went before the Civil Rights Commission. He stated that this conference was conducted on a highly professional and dignified basis. The opportunity to sit down in conference with a number of leading educators to discuss the problems involved in school desegregation was worthwhile. Mr. Oliver felt that his report on Nashville's desegregation was received with interest and respect. The next month Mr. Oliver and Board members A.B. Gibson, M.H. Pilsk, and T.C. Young attended a hearing before the U.S. District Court of Appeals in Cincinnati, Ohio regarding the desegregation suit. (Minutes, March 12 and May 14, 1959) The NAACP had appealed to this court when the District Court in Nashville approved the desegregation plans there. This court upheld the decision made in Nashville. The NAACP then attempted to appeal the case to the Supreme Court, but that court refused to review the case. (Henry Oliver to the author, July 9, 1975) Attorney Hunt received a letter from the Supreme Court dated December 14, 1959. "The petition for writ for certiorari is denied." This meant the suit could not be appealed to a higher court. This was judged to perpetuate rather than limit racial discrimination. (Minutes, January 21, 1960)

At the Board meeting on April 5, 1962, Mr. Oliver stated that he had been invited to attend the Civil Rights Commission's Fourth Annual Conference on "Problems of Segregation and Desegregation of Public Schools." The Commission would pay his expenses to come to Washington, D.C. on May 3 and 4. This was Mr. Oliver's third time to attend their conference. No other school system had been so honored to Mr. Oliver's knowledge. He went intending to conduct himself in a way that would reflect continued credit on Nashville City Schools and its methods of desegregation. (Minutes, April 5, 1962)

Members of the local NAACP attended the Board meetings several times with requests or petitions. On February 8, 1962 they brought a request to remove barriers that prevented African-Americans from attending Hume-Fogg Technical School, which was the only technical school in the city at the time. They petitioned the Board to admit all qualified students without regard to race as of September, 1962. At the August 16 Board meeting, the Instruction Committee and the Recreation and Vocational Committee presented their recommendations after having studied the request along with Mr. Oliver. "It is the judgment of your Superintendent that the court-approved plan of desegregation . . . applies to the Hume-Fogg Technical and Vocational High School also and that we should adhere strictly to this plan." Therefore, Mr. Oliver recommended a denial of the request which was subsequently granted. The letter requesting desegregation at Hume-Fogg implied a request for desegregation of evening classes for adults. The Superintendent felt that the evening program was not included in the plan. Nobody would be excluded from such classes because of race. As far as Mr. Oliver knew, no one had been excluded at any time for this reason. (Minutes, February 8 and August 16, 1962) Mrs. C.M. Hayes, a NAACP representative, came before the Board on March 21, 1963 asking for integration of Hume-Fogg, but it was still not granted. When the Transitional Board of Education governed both Nashville and Davidson County Schools, a revision struck from the books racial qualifications as a reason for transfer of a student to another school zone. (Minutes of Transitional Board, September 12 and June 13, 1963)

Certainly, Mr. Oliver was the guiding force behind the Desegregation Plan since Mr. Bass was ill much of the time when the Assistant Superintendent in essence acted as the Superintendent. So Henry Oliver dealt with the issue from the beginning. A study of the plan and the events over the years still leaves one without a thorough understanding of how Mr. Oliver really felt about the issue. He spoke a number of times on the subject. One of these speeches gives a picture of his opinions and feelings about desegregation. This speech was made to a group of concerned citizens from several organizations, some of which had the word Christian in their name. They met at the Clark Memorial Methodist Church. So he spoke as a Christian to other Christians. He stressed that people had to obey the edicts of the court. "I do not make the laws. I do not render court decisions. I work under them. My business is education, --not primarily segregation or desegregation, but education . . . for all the children of all the people of our city." He talked about avoiding disorder and confusion. Mr. Oliver praised the Police Department for helping restore and keep order. He thought it was very important that the parent have the right to decide where a child would go to school. "The person most vitally concerned with a child's welfare and happiness is the parent . . . . With the parent, the child comes first, or should, I think, always. The question which each parent should try to answer is 'What is best for my child?'" Henry Oliver stressed one of his paramount rules, that everyone should be treated with fairness, kindness, respect, and consideration. He cited the biblical teaching that God is no respecter of persons. Among Christians there is a common spiritual kinship which transcends differences of race, ancestry, nationality, or opinion. (Henry Oliver, "Registrations, Transfers, etc. as Christians, August 24, 1958, Oliver Collection) Again, one wonders what desegregation would have been like with a lesser man at the helm of Nashville City Schools.

Now, we look at other incidents that occurred while Mr. Oliver was Superintendent. Selections are varied in an attempt to give a composite picture.

Mr. Oliver made many major decisions to say nothing of minor ones. A glance over the Minutes of the Board show him considering anything from replacing old desks and cloth shades to hiring, firing, or retiring teachers. If Mr. Oliver did not open the meetings with prayer, someone else did. His Superintendent's Report was a part of every meeting where he usually included the Superintendent's Snapshot, something he initiated. The Snapshot informed or entertained as it briefly gave a picture of something important from one or more of the schools. Both students and teachers were featured. After the Snapshot, Mr. Oliver's report listed personnel to be hired, leaving, or retiring. He reported on the use of school buildings for other than school functions, on the status of school funds, and on school break-ins. Nashville City Schools had their own bookbindery, and Mr. Oliver reported on the work there. Attached to his report were reports on the School Health Service, Visiting Teacher and Attendance, and the Division of Vocational Education.

William Henry Oliver faithfully attended any meetings that would assist him in doing his job or in helping the schools. One such meeting he attended was the Regional Meeting of the American Association of School Administrators in 1958 in St. Louis, Missouri. (Minutes, May 14, 1959 and January 6, 1958) He also went to Indianapolis, Indiana to the Convention of the Regional Association of Secondary School Principals that year. In March of 1958 the Governor's Conference on Education Beyond High School convened in Nashville. As attendance was by invitation only, Mr. Oliver attended as an invited participant and a representative of Mayor West. Soon after, the Superintendent attended a meeting of a sub-committee Study Council of the Tennessee Superintendents' Conference where he served as the chairman. This sub-committee studied the question of merit raises as they affected teachers' salaries. On March 25, he went to a conference held at A and I State College (now Tennessee State University) to study plans for an expanded urban renewal program. The expansion of this program would affect a number of students. Mr. Oliver attended as an observer at an In-Service training for teachers of the severely mentally retarded at the end of the month because he wanted to learn as much as possible about the program. Mr. Oliver was again out of the office for In-Service for Nashville City Schools, March 31-April 2. The Annual Tennessee Superintendents' Conference was held in Gatlinburg in the fall of 1958 and yes, Mr. Oliver was present. (Minutes, April 9 and October 9, 1958)

The University of Tennessee in Knoxville sponsored a conference for Tennessee public school superintendents in the summer of 1959. "Your Superintendent had the honor of being the presiding officer during the final day of the program. Copies of the program showing the topics discussed will be made available to the members of the Board on their request." Governor Buford Ellington's White House Conference convened in Nashville in the fall of 1959. Mr. Oliver attended and heard reports on youth work and problems throughout the state. (Minutes, August 13 and November 5, 1959) Two years later, Mr. Oliver served as a member of the host committee for the White House Regional Conference on Education when it was held in Nashville. (Minutes, February 8, 1962)

Here's a thumbnail sketch of 1960. Nashville's Superintendent gave a report on using the National Teachers' Exam at the Tennessee Superintendents' Conference. He said, "We are the only city in the state using the examination." In April, Mr. Oliver met with Mr. Brown, Assistant Secretary of the U.S. Department of Labor, at the U.S. Courthouse in Nashville. They discussed the changes in employment, population, and manpower for the next decade as well as the vital part education would play in meeting the needs. At the next Board meeting, Mr. Oliver showed the Board charts he had used with Mr. Brown. (Minutes, January 21, October 13 and April 21, 1960) Mr. Oliver was invited by the National Education Association to be one of twenty-five educators to go to West Africa. He declined the invitation because the dates conflicted with duties as a member of the Southern Association of Schools and

Colleges Accreditation Board. (Minutes, December 14, 1961)

In addition to participating in such events in the world of education, Henry Oliver attended many local functions which are too numerous to mention, but it would be inappropriate to omit some speeches that provide a sampling of these functions.

Mr. Oliver spoke to a Negro City Council Parent Teacher Fellowship in the fall of 1957. This was shortly after desegregation began. He pointed out that education was not integration or segregation and that desegregation was a fact. He discussed buildings, teachers, equipment, and what students were learning. (Henry Oliver, Head School, October 2, 1957, Oliver Collection) He spoke on desegregation to the Community Relations Council in November. His emphasis was much like the speech just mentioned. (Henry Oliver, Christ Episcopal Church, November 19, 1957, Oliver Collection)

During 1958, Mr. Oliver gave two noteworthy speeches. He spoke about "The Place of the Private Music Teacher—in Education and Life." He said that place was rather important. (Henry Oliver, Music Teachers' Guild, January 19, 1958, Oliver Collection) Three months later he spoke on the "Privileges of a Teacher." "I almost asked for the privilege of appearing before you today . . . . I wished to bring you a word of greeting." His speech placed the teacher on a high plain and reflected the high standards this Superintendent wanted in his teachers.

You are the finest people that many of your pupils know . . . . You will teach them to be good and upright, self-respecting and respectable . . . . that every privilege has an accompanying responsibility . . . . to be reverent, God-fearing, religious in the truest sense of the word . . . to judge wisely among the voices that call and the hands that beckon to them to follow. . . . to be free men and women . . . . (Henry Oliver, Nashville Teachers' Association, April 18, 1958, Oliver Collection)

Courage was Mr. Oliver's topic when he spoke at a Kappa Delta Pi Annual Banquet in Clarksville, Tennessee where he was introduced by Mr. Earl Sexton, another Stewart County native. During this speech, he reminisced about his years at Southwestern Presbyterian University. He recalled wrestling matches and cross country runs of the track teams in which he participated. He also inspired and challenged his audience to overcome disadvantages and to stand for the right. (Henry Oliver, Austin Peay State University, January 26, 1959, Oliver Collection)

Professor Oliver's topic in Dover, Tennessee was "The Challenge of Better Education in Today's World." He began with "You had no way of knowing how much, wherever I have gone and whatever I have done, my heart has always been in Stewart County." He went on to talk about improvements in education and what a challenge it was to teach in the era already being called the Space Age. He advised the teachers to adjust to the speed and to use, not abuse, power. (Henry Oliver, Stewart County Teachers' Association, August 25, 1959, Oliver Collection)

"What is Our Community Doing to Prevent Juvenile Delinquency?" was Mr. Oliver's topic when he spoke to the Negro City Council Parent Teacher Association. He mentioned the home, school, and church as well as law enforcement officers and juvenile courts. His concluding remarks were about exemplary living and prayer. (Henry Oliver, November 24, 1959, Oliver Collection)

Henry Oliver spoke on "Beverage Alcohol" before the City-County Parent Teacher Association. He had been concerned about teenage drinking for years; he was not taking on a new topic. He was thankful for the group's concern and reviewed some of the steps they had taken in trying to protect youth from the greatest threat of all—beverage alcohol. He concluded with suggestions for further action. (Henry Oliver, April 5, 1960, Oliver Collection)

Mr. Oliver gave the commencement address at the third graduation of the Pearl High Evening Vocational School. His one word topic was "Work." One should work though tired and faced with impossibilities and handicaps. One should work even if betrayed as Jesus was." (Henry Oliver, May 25, 1961 Oliver Collection) Certainly, this man knew the value of work.

Numerous times Mr. Oliver spoke to inform groups of what was going on in the schools. He spoke to a group of executives at the Third National Bank on "Your Schools—Time for a Progress Report." Nashville had 44 schools, over 30,000 students, and 1,200 teachers. The speaker mentioned desegregation, educational television, federal aid, civil defense, and the future Metropolitan government. He gave this speech again at Napier Elementary School when they celebrated American Education Week. (Henry Oliver, November 1 and 9, 1961, Oliver Collection)

Henry Oliver was on WSM radio to inform the public about "Financial Support of Education." He talked about Metro which was little more than a year away. A matter of utmost concern was the school budget for 1963-64. He appealed for education to go forward, not backward, and it could do that only if the people voted for the increased budget. This new budget was $240,000 more than the current one. This program was sponsored by the Civic Committee on Education, which he commended. He reminded his audience that "The curse of public education in America is mediocrity and our greatest peril is public apathy. Our greatest need is for real concern, support, action on the part of the citizenry . . . ." (Henry Oliver, May 23, 1963, Oliver Collection)

Opportunities also came for Mr. Oliver to speak to student organizations. He addressed the Interhigh Student Council which met at West End High School on "The Value of Student Leadership." (Henry Oliver, January 14, 1963, Oliver Collection.) In addition, he spoke at the Metropolitan Nashville Future Teachers' Association's Awards Banquet, taking as his topic "A Poem, A Picture, and A Purpose." He called to his listeners' attention the personal satisfaction that comes through service that a teacher renders. (Henry Oliver, April 30, 1964, Oliver Collection)

Three new programs were introduced in Nashville during Mr. Oliver's time at the helm, which were in place for years. These included tuition-free summer school, kindergarten, and educational television which were considered major advances in education.

Tentative plans were made for a summer school without tuition in 1958 but did not materialize. The plan would have offered refresher courses in English and mathematics. Due to developments in connection with the budget, the Superintendent did not ask the Board to approve the plan. Davidson County Schools had a similar program with financial assistance from the Ford Foundation. Mr. Oliver asked for permission to work with the Superintendent of county schools in an effort to allow a limited number of city school students to participate in the county's program and this request was approved.

The Instruction Committee considered the Superintendent's request for an expanded program of summer school work in the spring of 1959. Such a program would prevent a waste of time for both students and teachers. The plan would involve remedial work for elementary schools as well as make-up work for high school students. Enrichment programs would provide opportunity for the gifted and ambitious student. The committee approved Mr. Oliver's request, asked for the concurrence of the Board, and the Board granted its approval. (Minutes, March 12, 1959)

Tentative plans were drawn up. The Superintendent asked for permission to employ about fifty teachers with a budget of $20,000. More than 11,000 students could have attended the session. This many students could not be accommodated at that time. Thus, priorities were set. Remedial high school work was top priority with enrichment on that level being the second consideration. Remedial work on the elementary level came in third while enrichment at that level was last on the continuum. Remedial work would be mainly in basic academic areas like English, social sciences, and mathematics. The enrichment courses would include such courses as typing, art, and foreign language. If a student was a bonafide resident of the city, there would be no charge. The Board approved the plan as described. However, they were unable to have a summer session in all four areas as listed. The Superintendent was authorized to permit summer programs for the first three grades where requests were made and where circumstances justified a program. Tuition was to be charged for these programs. (Minutes, April 9 and May 14, 1959)

Summer school in 1960 was an improvement over summer school in 1959. Tuition-free summer school opened for grades one through twelve with over 2,400 students attending. For the first six grades, the program was entirely remedial work. Grades seven through twelve had both make-up and enrichment classes. A large percentage of summer school students had perfect attendance and over ninety-five percent passed their courses. Scores of students were able to finish high school a year earlier because of this summer session. Mr. Oliver personally visited every classroom in the program. "We know that good work was done." Music was offered but on a tuition basis. (Minutes, August 11, 1960) The 1961 program added three full-time teachers who taught driver training. (Minutes, May 11, 1961)

"THEREFORE BE IT RESOLVED, that the Nashville Board of Education in regular session January 9, 1958 memorializes the Tennessee School Boards' Association to request the State to set up similar funds for kindergartens and to formulate a plan by which local Boards of Education may use these satisfactorily." (Minutes, January 9, 1958) The State did not heed this resolution for several years for it was four years before Nashville had a limited summer kindergarten program and in the fall Pilot Kindergartens were established. The time has come, when the City of Nashville should undertake some sort of kindergarten . . . . except at Oak Ridge, there are no public kindergartens in Tennessee . . . no State funds are available . . . we should consider inaugurating such a program on our own. Nashville has long led the State . . . and the South, and our school system has been an outstanding one.

Mr. Oliver expressed appreciation for the Mayor's interest this letter showed. (Minutes, January 18, 1962)

The "Proposed Plan for a Summer Kindergarten Program" was presented by the Instruction Committee at the February Board meeting and passed as submitted. The program was to last eight weeks, employ teachers in the system, and be supervised by Dr. L.J. Willis, who was the Supervisor of Elementary Education. It was tuition-free and open to students eligible for the first grade in the fall of 1962. A teacher's salary was $400 for the session, with double pay if one taught a class in morning and afternoon. Class size ranged from twenty to twenty-five. The estimated cost of $12,000 was included in the Summer School Budget. Enrollment of a child was voluntary with classes in all elementary schools in the city. About 1600 students enrolled and were taught by sixty-eight teachers. In March, the Board members voted to have Pilot Kindergarten Programs for the 1962-1963 term. These were in the following schools: Hattie Cotton, Meigs, Buena Vista, Sylvan Park and Clemons. (Minutes, February 8, April 5 and August 16, 1962)

William Henry Oliver first mentioned educational television in 1958. In his opinion, it had great possibilities. He did not ask for any action from the Board then; he only asked them to consider the factors involved. (Minutes, April 9, 1958) Three years later, the Instruction Committee after careful consideration made a recommendation on the matter. Recognizing television as an important medium of education, they stated that if a station was to operate successfully, it must be largely supported by public funds. Rather than subsidize a program, the Board thought it best to own and operate a station.

> We recommend that the Board . . . make application as soon as is practical for a license to own and operate an educational television station on Channel 2. We also recommend that the Davidson County Board . . . join us in this application in order that the two Boards . . . may own, support, manage, and operate the station jointly. We recommend too that local educational institutions such as Vanderbilt, Peabody, etc. as well as other school systems within the area . . . be participants . . . . (Minutes, January 19, 1961)

Both City and County Committees were appointed to work on plans for educational television. The City Committee consisted of Mr. Elmer Pettit, Mr. Gibson and Mr. Oliver. The County Committee consisted of Mr. Olin White, Mr. Ed Chappel, and Superintendent Moss. The cost of installation was to be shared by the two Boards on a 50-50 basis with operating costs divided on an Average Daily Attendance basis. Earnest efforts were made to secure donations and contributions from commercial television stations and groups of citizens. Vanderbilt gave $50,000 toward the construction and installation of Channel 2. The Nashville Board had funds available for the purchase of equipment and the construction of facilities. The results of a study of the Atlanta educational television program were available to members of the committees. Channel 2 was not to compete with commercial stations, but it would make available programs for rebroadcast on commercial stations.

There would be no advertising, no religious services as such, no political broadcasting, and no fund raising.

Mr. Oliver gave a report on educational television to the Board in April of 1961. Though progress was not quite as fast as he would have liked, it was satisfactory. The legal services of Kirkland, Ellis, Hodson, Chaffetz, and Masters in Washington, D.C were secured. Attorneys had drawn up a legal agreement between the city and county to show joint ownership and operation. Request was made to WSIX for land on their hill for locating a tower and transmitter. (Minutes, February 23 and April 17, 1961)

The Joint Committee on Educational Television chose Andrew McMaster as Chief Engineer at a salary of $8,000 a year to begin November 1, 1961. The Board approved this and the offer of $150,000 to WSM for facilities located near Belmont College. This included the tower, building and grounds. Terms were reached and the WSM property was purchased. The construction permit include the suggested call letters of WNDC, WDCN, WAOS, WMTE, and WEND. Hart, Freeland, and Roberts were selected as the architects for the transmitter. Robert Glazier was the first station manager with an annual salary of $11,000. (Minutes, July 27, November 9, December 14, and August 10, 1961)

The Board of Education acted on several recommendations concerning educational television in 1962. They voted to become an affiliate of the National Educational Television network and paid the $9,000 annual fee. The main benefit from this affiliation was a $60,000 videotape recorder. Also, the affiliation made available programs from sixty-two educational television stations across the country. The Board approved a plan to invite outlying school systems to participate in educational television by contributing fifty-five cents per pupil based on Average Daily Attendance toward the first year's operating budget for Channel 2.

The April report of the Joint Committee on Educational Television stated that the application to the Federal Communications Commission had been approved. By the flip of a coin, the call letters of WDCN (Davidson County-Nashville) were chosen instead of WNDC (Nashville-Davidson County). In June "installation of transmitter and master control equipment is nearing completion, and the old WSM-TV Channel 4 antenna will be replaced by a new WDCN-TV Channel 2 antenna atop the 500 foot tower at 15th and Compton this weekend." Experimental test telecasts were aired during the week of June 24. This qualified WDCN for $50,000 in state matching funds for 1961-1962. (Minutes, March 8, April 5 and June 14, 1962)

Other moves affected the educational world during 1957-1964 but did not continue into the present. One that readily comes to mind is the Civil Defense Program. In 1957, Kathryn Millspaugh, Dr. L.J. Willis, and John Oliver went to Atlanta to observe the evacuation of students as directed by the Civil Defense Authorities. In 1958 and 1959 Nashville Schools participated in the planned pupil evacuation directed by the Nashville-Davidson County Civil Defense. Robert Dunkerley represented the City Schools early in 1962 at a discussion of proposed plans for civil defense as these related to schools. When he reported to the Board, it ended civil defense as a part of the school program. (Minutes, November 14, 1957, September 10, 1959 and

February 8, 1962) Another matter that didn't continue was setting up a special adjustment room designed to keep boys from becoming dropouts. Courses were determined by what was practical, of interest and their aptitudes. The program was for fifteen and sixteen year old boys. In the 1960-1961 term it apparently worked for the limited number in the class. (Minutes, August 11, 1960) The Transitional Board eliminated this class for maladjusted boys to alleviate overcrowded buildings and to adjust the budget to provide more free lunches. (Minutes of Transitional Board, September 12, 1963, hereafter referred to as Transitional)

One matter that caused far-reaching effects and continues to influence public education today was a Supreme Court decision. In 1963, the Transitional Board appointed a special committee to study the ruling on Bible reading and prayer in public schools. Superintendents Oliver and Moss along with Attorney Merritt served on this committee. The first statement the committee made did not exclude prayer. Mr. Oliver felt that he could not exclude prayer. His thoughts were that the government could just put him in jail or whatever, but he would pray. The Board did not pass on it as written and asked that the statement be rewritten because they were afraid of the consequences of not complying completely. (Henry Oliver to the author, July 9, 1975) The Board adopted the second statement. The most direct legal interpretation they could obtain said that the Supreme Court had ruled against State-required Bible reading or prayer. There had been a State law requiring the reading of a certain number of verses from the Bible each day. The ruling of the Court made this law null and void. The Constitution, as interpreted by the Supreme Court, permits voluntary or individual prayer by students. Teachers should not conduct or supervise public prayer in public schools, although periods of meditation or silent prayer were permitted. Nothing in any law forbade the reading of inspirational literature, including the Bible, for educational or moral purposes. "The teacher should not, however, read any literature as a part of a religious exercise or worship service in the public schools." (Transitional, September 5, 1963)

Shortly thereafter, Mr. Oliver spoke at the Free Will Baptist Pastors' Conference on the "Implications of Supreme Court Ruling on Bible Reading and Prayer." This speech is the true gauge of his opinions on this ruling. He stated that it was inconsistent with American ideals as well as being a misinterpretation of the Constitution. He went further to say it was a victory for communism and that it reflected a lack of dependence on God plus no belief in prayer. (Henry Oliver, January 20, 1964, Oliver Collection)

In 1959, high school principals were notified that they were at liberty to have programs planned by the Middle Tennessee Mental Health Association during Mental Health Week. This started real change in guidance and special education. Soon, the Psychology Department of Tennessee A and I University (now Tennessee State University) offered three well-qualified students to administer individual intelligence tests at certain African-American schools. Since school psychologists had too much work, this assistance was appreciated. The same year the Superintendent was authorized to use the financial assistance available in the field of guidance through the Federal Defense Act. (Minutes, March 12, April 9 and June 11, 1959) The next year guidance rooms at West, North, and Howard Schools were remodeled. Now guidance counselors had private rooms for the first time. Equipment for the rooms was obtained through the National Defense Educational Act. A few months later the

Board voted to grant the Superintendent permission to look for a person to coordinate the guidance program and for three secretarial workers for the program. Benjamin Allen was the school psychologist and Director of the Student Testing Program for most of Mr. Oliver's years as Superintendent. Mr. Allen spoke to the Board as the Snapshot in 1961 where he discussed and illustrated his program. (Minutes, January 21 and December 15, 1960 and November 9, 1961) Advocates for the guidance program were glad to have their program before the Board.

Mr. Oliver made decisions regarding special education while he was Superintendent. Special education here refers to any instruction provided other than that for the average child in a typical classroom. Only one reference was found regarding the gifted child. Two classes were set up in the fall of 1963 for the most gifted from all the elementary schools. The size ranged from twelve to eighteen per class. Two different plans were practiced. In one plan, only fourth graders were enrolled. In the other class, students from third through sixth grades were enrolled. Those students identified as gifted from each grade reported to the special education teacher one day each week for enrichment instruction. (Minutes, April 5, 1962)

The program for the mentally retarded and/or the physically handicapped changed and several classes were added between 1957-1964. The program for the severely retarded children moved from the Vine Hill Housing Project (Edgehill) to the Buena Vista School in the fall of 1958. Buena Vista had a physical therapist provided for students with cerebral palsy by the fall of 1959. The Parents' Council for Cerebral Palsy paid for this service. The maximum number of pupils permitted in a severely retarded classroom was eighteen. The average number of pupils in an educable mentally retarded classroom was twenty. There was a backlog of twenty to thirty children who needed to be in the severely retarded class and about forty of these students who should have been in the educable mentally retarded classes were in regular classrooms. The program had these seven divisions:

    Educable Mentally Retarded
    29 teachers

    Speech and Hearing
    7 teachers

    Homebound
    4 teachers

    Partially-Seeing
    3 teachers

    Cerebral Palsy
    3 teachers

    Severely Mentally Retarded
    3 teachers

    Hospital
    2 teachers

A considerable part of the special education program was carried on in cooperation with Davidson County Schools. The cerebral palsy and the sight-saving classes were done in cooperation with the county. (Minutes, September 11 and October 8, 1958) In 1960, two teachers were provided for emotionally disturbed children in

Vanderbilt Hospital. The State Department of Education paid their salaries. (Minutes, June 9, 1960) A year later a program for this group was instituted as a Pilot Project at Warner School which was a cooperative effort between the school systems, the State, and the Mental Health Center. Plans were made to open two more classes for elementary educable mentally retarded students. One was opened at McKissack and the other at Murrell. (Minutes, April 17 and March 9, 1961)

What was modern equipment at the time brought changes in education. These extended from the Superintendent's office to many classrooms. Mr. Oliver's office was to be properly furnished and decorated in early 1958. (Minutes, February 13 1958) These plans included a beautiful new desk, but Mr. Oliver declined the offer of carpet. He did not want to have things better than the rest of the staff and others weren't offered carpet. (Henry Oliver to the author, July 9, 1975) The Board authorized the purchase of a portable Dictaphone for the Superintendent's office. (Minutes, February 9, 1960)

The National Defense Educational Act of 1958 made it possible for Nashville City Schools to purchase much new equipment. In 1959, the Finance Committee recommended that the Board authorize the Superintendent to file application for participation in the expenditure of funds made available through this Act. The Board so voted. The State Department of Education approved the application. And $17,500 of federal money was made available for equipment and materials. The city was required to match this amount. First, the funds purchased equipment and materials in science, mathematics, and modern foreign languages. The total spent for equipment that first year was over $33,000;

most of this was used for audio-visual equipment and materials, work tables, and storage cabinets. The total spent over three years was $224,576.75. (Minutes, May 14 and June 11, 1959 and March 9, 1961)

The U.S. Department of Commerce installed equipment in three Nashville schools. These were triangulation stations at Caldwell, Howard, and Ford-Greene. These were used in connection with the coast and geodetic survey.

In December of 1960, the City School System purchased an electronic stencil cutter for $1,800, half of which came from federal funds. Two years later the first twenty electric typewriters were purchased for typing classes. (Minutes, June 11, 1959, December 15, 1960 and October 22, 1962) Many more advances were made during the transitional years. Recommendations for Metro included a plan to establish a modern system of data processing in the Business Affairs Office which came to fruition. The initial equipment purchases consisted of key punch, verifier, sorter with counter, accounting machine, and interpreter. (Transitional, February 25, 1964) Had the computer era arrived?

Language laboratories in two senior high schools were planned in 1961. Teaching of foreign languages at the elementary level was encouraged as far as the capabilities of the teachers permitted. (Minutes, May 11, 1961)

Imagine for a moment that you are a teacher in Nashville during these years. What added benefits were available? How were the classes and methods of instruction changed? What disciplinary measures were practiced?

First, consider the resources available. An efficient curriculum department provided notable resource units for Nashville teachers. One was "The Beginnings of the Space Age." The Superintendent received a complimentary letter from the U.S. Commissioner of Education, Dr. Lawrence Derthick, regarding this unit. He was particularly pleased with the approach. Consultants, or teachers, were provided to assist teachers in all subject areas. The teacher-pupil ratio was just below thirty in 1959. (Minutes, August 16, 1958, and June 11, October 8 and November 5, 1959) The community resource program gave teachers ample opportunity to enrich their classes. Mr. Oliver had a taped interview with the editor of *School Management* concerning this program in 1960. The information was used in an article titled "How to Tap Community Resources for Your School" in the magazine. The article communicated valuable ideas to other school systems. Nashville was one of eleven school systems in the country that was chosen by the Ford Foundation's National Music Council for the placement of a young composer. This provided a unique opportunity for music teachers. This individual worked closely with music supervisors and teachers. Primary teachers received special assistance in teaching reading. Outstanding reading teachers served as roving teachers for the first eight weeks of school to assist teachers in grades one through three.

Second, consider the benefits available. Teachers were eligible to participate in social security in 1958. They could retire with a pension after twenty years of service instead of twenty-five. Vocational teachers were employed on a ten calendar months basis. The salary scale in 1962 started teachers with bachelor degrees at $4,000 annually. The maximum after fifteen years of experience was $5,940. Differentials of nine points or $360 were offered for each succeeding degree through the Ph.D. Supplements for teachers of special subjects were increased ten percent. A special incentive was given to teachers who supervised a student teacher during the school year. Peabody College and the City Schools had an agreement that allowed for teachers to take courses at no charge. At the last meeting of the Nashville Board of Education, Mr. Oliver mentioned many of these benefits. He mentioned life insurance and hospitalization which was provided for teachers. Teachers were granted sabbatical and professional leaves. Military service time could also count toward a teacher's retirement. (Minutes, December 16, 1957, August 10, 1961, July 17 and 19, October 11, 1962 and September 8, 1960)

Third, consider the methods of instruction used in this era. Keep in mind that new equipment, especially audio-visuals, and resources available were related to the methods of instruction. From 1958-1961, Warner had a non-graded primary unit program which began as a Pilot Study. The principal, R.N. Chenault, presented a report on the program that pleased Mr. Oliver. Team teaching was another method of instruction used. The non-graded classroom continued for longer than the team teaching classroom. East Nashville Junior High had an experimental project using team teaching when the school opened in 1961. Wharton used a modified team teaching project for sixth grade the same year. Teachers who participated in these experiments did make changes in methods of instruction. (Minutes, August 10, July 27 and October 12, 1961)

Disciplinary measures from 1957-1964 will be the last area examined. Teachers were urged to discipline through kindness and persuasive means, but if these failed, there was an alternative. If a teacher had the written permission of the parent and the principal, corporal punishment could be administered. When it was used, it had to be promptly reported to the principal and the principal had to include it in his monthly report to the superintendent. Self-discipline was expected of all teachers. They were to abstain from using tobacco in the presence of their students. School parties, games, or any school sponsored function had to be properly chaperoned. Mr. Oliver was complimented highly on the way he handled teacher conduct. (Minutes, January 19, 1961)

What changes did students notice from 1957-1964? Of course, resources, disciplinary actions, methods of instruction and equipment used affected students. However, other changes were made that are worth mentioning. Graduation requirements and diplomas changed. At the Superintendent's suggestion, one unit of science was required beginning in 1958. In June, 1959, students began receiving a diploma showing the subjects taken. This plan was used rather than issuing a college preparatory and a non-college preparatory diploma. The expressions "cum laude" and "magna cum laude" were added. (Minutes, May 8, 1958)

Elementary students saw changes as well. Fifth graders first received New Testaments from the Gideons in 1959. That class also participated in a "Learn-to-Swim" program. These lessons were given during school hours at pools provided by local agencies. About 250 students participated.

Musically inclined students were fortunate to live in Nashville. "Your Superintendent feels that music is a very important part of the curriculum . . . ." It was not considered a "frill." The Board of Education owned a rather large number of musical instruments. The Superintendent could remember when there was not a single horn nor one band director employed in the city. Every student had the opportunity to be involved in the music program. The system was one of the few that had stringed instruments. Nashville City Schools were cited as having a "balanced music program."

Married students had certain rules they had to obey. A husband and wife could not attend the same school. They could not take part in interscholastic competitive activities including athletics. Within one week after the wedding, the student had to report to the principal or guidance counselor for counseling and a discussion of rules applying to them. Failure to do so could result in immediate dismissal from school. (Minutes, April 9, May 14 and August 13, 1959)

What about younger students? They must have profited from the emphasis placed on the reading program. Mr. M.D. Neely, Assistant Supervisor of Elementary Education, brought some African-American first graders to the Board meeting in 1960. They demonstrated the success of concentrated efforts to improve the teaching of reading in primary grades. Mr. Oliver states that "nothing else is so vital to formal education as the teaching of reading. The ability to read is the key which unlocks the door to the future in the scholastic career of every boy and girl."

Look back at high school students now. From the students' standpoint, a significant course, Drivers' Education, was added in some schools and expanded in others at this time. The Superintendent said, "The time is ripe for the launching of an all-out effort . . . to make Nashville the safest city in America . . . ." The Mayor and City Council made available ample funds for this course. The best equipment was purchased from Drivotrainers. An article appeared in the *Drivotrainers Digest* in 1961 about the Nashville program. (Minutes, July 14 and September 8, 1960; April 17, 1961)

Both sixth graders and other elementary students took part in a plan to improve penmanship. A project in which all students participated was helping to select a flag for the city of Nashville. Sixth graders were excited in 1960 when the Superintendent made arrangements for twenty-eight sixth grade classes to take part in a television science program made available through the County School System. Students received certificates for successfully completing the sixth grade beginning in the 1960-1961 term. (Minutes, April 21, October 13 and November 17, 1960; March 8, 1962)

One change that affected some students at all levels was the free lunch program. In 1962, the School Board provided $460,000 to pay for lunches for children unable to pay. Applicants were rigidly screened and rigid economics were practiced in managing and operating school lunchrooms. Schools were strongly urged to go under the national Lunch Program. (Minutes, October 11, 1962 and Transitional, September 4, 1963)

The Manpower Development and Training act affected older students as well as some adults. The Superintendent recommended that Nashville take part in this program which provided training for the unemployed and under-employed. The local school board made buildings available while the State Department of Education purchased all necessary equipment and supplies as well as paying the instructors and funding the operating costs of the program. Mechanical drafting was the first course offered. (Minutes, June 14, 1962)

In early 1964, steps were initiated to offer classes for eighteen year olds who were illiterate. Expenses were to be paid by the State. Class size ranged from ten to thirty. The Board elected the teacher who served at five dollars per hour for about three hours a week. (Transitional, December 9, 1963)

This section on the activities during Mr. Oliver's years as superintendent is only a thumbnail sketch, for much has been left unsaid. In speaking to the last city Board of Education, Mr. Oliver gave a concise summary of these years. Wharton, McKissack, Murrell, Johnson and perhaps other schools had opened. Knox, Lipscomb, Lockeland Annex, Tarbox, and Ford-Greene had closed. Technical and vocational programs had expanded. Other items mentioned have been covered in this section. A few months later that Board met for the last time. Mr. Oliver reported that the contract was being let for the West Nashville Junior High School. He expected that one would be let within three years for the Rose Park Junior High School. The addition to Highland Heights was almost complete and plans were for an addition to West End Senior High School. He asked that he be authorized to prepare, immediately, plans for additions and new buildings to relieve the overcrowded conditions at Pearl Senior, Wharton, Washington, Ford-Greene and McKissack. In a summary at the same meeting, he talked about the fine vocational programs at Pearl and Hume-Fogg. These schools also had a fine practical nurses program. Furthermore, library services, which included a professional library for teachers, were outstanding in the system. Finally, they were spending $100,000 for guidance services that year. (Minutes, January 18 and October 11, 1962)

Attention is now turned to the consolidation of the City and County School Systems. The Commissioner of Education called a meeting early in 1961. H.H. Turpen, Assistant Superintendent in charge of finance, attended. Seven members from both the city and county boards were to serve on a committee to study the school situations and make recommendations. Before any recommendations could become law, they were subject to approval by the City Council and the County Court. The bill had to be presented to the people in the form of a referendum. In just a little over a year, copies of the charter proposed for the metropolitan government were available to school board members. They were instructed by their Superintendent to take particular note of transitional provisions regarding public schools. (Minutes, February 9, 1961 and April 5, 1962) The City School System which had existed for over a hundred years would cease to exist.

The work of the Transitional Board of Education, or the Interim Metro Board as it was sometimes called, is now discussed. This Board existed from October of 1962 until July of 1964. It first met on October 18 with Dr. Henry Hill serving as chairman. Other members were Mrs. Tom Bland, Mr. E.C. Carman, E.D. Chappel, Dr. Walter S. Davis, A.B. Gibson, Elmer Pettit, Frank P. White and S.L. Wright. At these meetings, separate city and county reports were presented by the superintendents on many matters. Joint reports were given when possible. The Board rotated its meeting place between the county's headquarters on Bransford Avenue and the city's headquarters in the Hume-

Fogg Building on Broadway. (Transitional, October 28, 1962 and March 21 1963)

To complete a comprehensive survey of the two systems was one of the major jobs of the Transitional Board. After several offers were made, the contract went to Educational Research Services of White Plains, New York. Dr. Francis G. Cornell served as the educational consultant. The cost of the survey was $36,000. Four hundred copies of the complete survey were printed and 20,000 copies of the summary were published. Results of this survey are presented when recommendations for Metro are discussed.

In October of 1963, a progress report summarized the efforts toward merging the two systems. Supervisors were urged to think of the systems as one. The superintendents had laid the groundwork for a spirit of unity among all the employees. Everyone in both systems was working together and looking forward to the merger being complete by July 1, 1964.

The Steering Committee played an important part in merger plans. The committee was composed of A.E. Wright, F.A. Detchon, J.K. Brown, R.F. Gruber and Dr. A.K. Klein. The two superintendents appointed the Policies Committee to compare the policies of the two systems. The superintendents usually met with these committees and the other ones working toward the merger. (Transitional, October 10 and 24, 1963; June 25 1964)

There is not a discussion of the many decisions of this Board concerning general matters. Keep in mind though that all the usual details of a large school system were handled even though the Board spent long hours working on the merger of the two systems. This should give one a great appreciation for the individuals involved in the work of those years.

By February, 1964, recommendations for Metro were ready. The Board adopted an administrative organization which had a Director of Schools as the chief administrator. This person was to have an academic background showing breadth and depth. "The doctorate is desired." Experience both as a teacher and a superintendent was required. The budget set the salary for the Director at $20,000. Four major administrative divisions would each be under an Associate Director of Schools. These divisions were Instruction, Professional Services, Business Affairs and School Transportation and Physical Facilities. The Division of Instruction included General Education, Special Education, Adult and Vocational Education and Educational Television. Within the Division of Professional Services were the departments of Personnel, Research and Development, Instructional Materials, Pupil Personnel Services and Public School Health Services. Accounting and Finance, Purchasing and Supply, Data Processing and School Lunch Services were a part of the Division of Business Affairs. Three departments of the Division of School Transportation and Physical Facilities were School Transportation, Building Construction, and School Plant Operation and Maintenance. A recommendation passed for an administrative assistant to represent the Director on many occasions. This person was to be sensitive to public concerns and capable of explaining all phases of the school system to groups and individuals. A month later the Board voted for the 1964-1965 Metro operating budget to be $33,607,008.

One act of the Transitional Board had nothing to do with Metro, but it is pertinent here. At the May meeting members of the Board voted unanimously to name East Nashville High School's new gymnasium the William Henry Oliver Gymnasium. (Transitional, February 25 and May 28, 1964)

The Transitional Board assembled for the last time in June of 1964. William Henry Oliver presented a report prepared by him and Superintendent Moss. He commended the Board members sincerely for a job well done. "Any certificate or diploma that you may receive as you complete your task would bear the inscription 'summa cum laude.'" (Transitional, June 25, 1964) The 300 page *Comprehensive Survey of the Metropolitan School System* was completed and accepted by the Board in October, 1963. When the Board began to implement the Survey recommendations, it was clear that the Steering Committee and various sub-committees needed professional help in resolving knotty problems. Dr. E.C. Merrill, Dean, University of Tennessee, was retained as a consultant. In addition, four well-qualified educators were chosen as special consultants for the merger. These were Dr. Ben Carmichael, Superintendent of Chattanooga Schools; Dr. John Letsen, Superintendent of Atlanta City Schools; Dr. James Whitlock, Associate Director, Division of Surveys and Field Services, Peabody College; and Dr. E.C. Stimbert, Superintendent of Memphis City Schools. These specialists, the Board, the superintendents, the Steering Committee along with some thirty odd sub-committees resolved many of the problems connected with merging. And so it was that the Transitional Board turned over to the Metro Board and Metro Director on July 1, 1964 a 90,000-pupil school system with personnel and physical facilities consolidated.

Portraits of both Superintendents, Oliver and Moss, were to hang in the Board of Education room forever. That was not to be the case. A group including a 1956 graduate of East Nashville High, Ed Birthright, acquired funds to have a portrait artist paint Mr. Oliver. It did hang in the offices on Bransford Avenue until the building was remodeled. The painting of Mr. Oliver disappeared and has not been located. It is unknown how old Mr. Oliver was in the picture from which the portrait was painted. Interestingly, the portrait of Mr. Moss is still somewhere in the building on Bransford Avenue. (Edward Birthright to the author, October 22, 2015)

Former superintendent of Nashville City Schools had his portrait painted from a picture made years earlier. Here he sits with his beloved wife's photo on her piano in their home.

This is the picture from which the artist, Sherry Oats, painted the portrait. The portrait was a 16" by 20" oil painting on linen. The cover of this book was designed from a picture of the portrait which cannot be located.

Mr. Oliver with Ed Birthright, East High Class of 1956, who was on the committee that commissioned the portrait.

This is a picture of the portrait.

Photos from Ed Birthright

Chapter 6

THE APEX

(1964-1991)

William Henry Oliver retired from public education in the fall of 1964 at the age of sixty. He had decided that he wanted no position with Metro. A large framed certificate of appreciation which the office staff presented upon his retirement hung in the hall of his home. The staff tried to describe the attributes of this man who had given thirty-four years of his life to education in the city of Nashville. This certificate contained the signatures of all members of the staff. Mr. Oliver and Mr. Moss actually acted as Co-Directors of Metro for about a month because as of July 1 no Director had been hired. Mr. Oliver retired one day and went back to work the next in 1964. As an Associate Professor, Mr. Oliver taught in the Education and English Departments at Belmont College (now University) in Nashville,

Tennessee. He supervised the secondary student teachers until the spring of 1969.

During Mr. Oliver's last year at Belmont, he served as the General Chairman for the Self-Study. He stated that each department was so cooperative in preparing its report that his task was much easier. This Self-Study was the regular ten year study required of all colleges accredited by the Southern Association of Colleges and Secondary Schools, as Belmont was already accredited. (Henry Oliver to the author, July 5 and July 25, 1974) All of Belmont's faculty and twenty-eight students were involved. There were eight committees who worked on the 281 page study.

According to Dr. Herbert C. Gabhart, Belmont's president at the time, Mr. Oliver expressed an interest in coming to Belmont as early as 1960 or 1961. Professor Oliver brought prestige to Belmont's Education Department. He possessed strength of character and was diligent and dependable. He was a good organizer, as evidenced in his capable direction of Belmont's Self Study in 1969-1970. He understood the administration and always cooperated with it. Many times he placed himself in a position to assist; that is, he volunteered to do whatever he could to help. He was respected by his students. Because Mr. Oliver was always trying to learn more in order to do more, he took Education 520 at Peabody in the summer of 1964. Assuredly, William Henry Oliver was a senior statesman in the area of education. (Dr. Herbert C. Gabhart to the author, November 29, 1974)

Professor Oliver of Belmont College often spoke on education to various groups. Mr. Oliver spoke on "Religion and the Public Schools" to the Baptist Student Union at Peabody College in 1964. He spoke as an American

Christian citizen, not as a representative of Metro Schools, from which he was leaving, nor of Belmont, to which he was going. He reviewed the history of religion and its involvement in education. He mentioned the Supreme Court's ruling concerning religion in public schools which was covered in chapter 5. He closed with, "Obey the law as long as it is law; change it if you desire." (Henry Oliver, July 21, 1964, Oliver Collection)

Dr. John Harper Harris, Director of Metro Schools, asked Mr. Oliver to speak to the Metro staff in the spring of 1965. He spoke on the sales tax issue at Lentz Health Center. Henry Oliver told Dr. Harris that he would stay out of his way, but would be anxious to help him if he needed his assistance. He did not tell others how to vote. Because of his deep interest in public education and urgent need for additional funds, he was for an increased sales tax which would be used for education. (Henry Oliver, July 21 and May 10, 1965, Oliver Collection)

The dedication of the William Henry Oliver Building at East High School was a great occasion for Mr. Oliver. He gave a short response after G.H. Waters gave the dedication address. He was surrounded by friends and overwhelmed by memories on that December day.

> Most men to whom buildings are dedicated are dead before the dedication ceremonies take place. So I'm thankful to be here, *Alive*. I am thankful also that Mrs. Oliver is able to be here. Six months ago the doctors would not have predicted that she would be . . . . People are always saying nicer things about me than I deserve. I wish that I could be worthy of them all. . . I take little credit for the progress that

was made . . . . Finally, my friends, let me express again my deep, humble, and sincere thanks for the special honor which is mine tonight in having this beautiful building bear my name.

He appreciated the twenty-five wonderful years at East and his seven years as superintendent.

Perhaps, no other speech is more representative of William Henry Oliver's character. This response shows so clearly his humility, his sincerity, and his appreciation for life with all its variety. And as the dedication caption stated, he was "one whose Life Has Been Unusually Blessed and Unselfishly Useful." (Henry Oliver, December 3, 1965, Oliver Collection)

"Speaking on television is not a new experience for me, but speaking, for what might be considered a political purpose is new for me—completely new." Mr. Oliver thus opened his part on a live television show in 1966. The speech, "Ben West and Education," was given on WLAC when Ben West ran for Mayor of Metro. Mayor West's attitude toward schools had been one of interest, concern, and support; not one of interference or control. "He consistently supported me and the Board of Education financially, approving each year additional expenditures for education from local funds." He gave to them consistent confidence and support and to him "I shall be eternally grateful." (Henry Oliver, Summer, 1966, Oliver Collection)

On May 26, 1966, the Olivers and Mrs. McCall, Pauline's Mother, planned to come to Stewart County High School for the author's graduation. However, Mrs. Oliver had just been diagnosed with Alzheimer's. In line to graduate, Principal Van Riggins came to the author to express Mr. Oliver's regrets that he could not attend. This shows the thoughtfulness of this gentleman. Previously, doctors had thought that Mrs. Oliver might have a tumor on the front part of her brain. After two or three weeks of tests, the doctors decided on surgery. Henry had noticed that Pauline's memory, which had always been sharp, was failing. The surgery revealed no tumor and afterwards, her condition was diagnosed as Alzheimer's, a gradual deterioration of the central nervous system. (Henry Oliver to the author, July 9, 1975)

Henry had different caregivers in their home. One of these was Marie Oliver Stepp who called him "Uncle Henry." They were related but the uncle was a term of love and respect for him. During the time the author spent in their home when she was working on the original book, Mrs. Oliver's face would light up when he entered the room. She passed away in August of 1977.

"Improving Student-Faculty Relations" was Mr.Oliver's topic to the Belmont faculty in 1968. Generally speaking, the relationship between teachers and students was good at Belmont. This was partly due to the fact that both faculty and students were, for the most part, Christians. The value of communication was emphasized. "Whatever ideas I may have . . . are of little, or no value, unless I can communicate them to my students . . . . Between us and today's college generation there is a gulf which cannot be removed. The best we can do is to try . . . . to bridge it with kindness, concern, and understanding." Teachers should show their concern for students' activities. This is done by attending student functions.

William Henry Oliver spoke at a Six County In-Service meeting at Waverly, Tennessee in August of 1968. The counties represented were Humphreys, Hickman, Houston, Dickson, Perry, and Stewart. Mr. Oliver gave the keynote address at the General Session after being introduced by Mr. Lathan Keatts, another native of Stewart County, from the State Department of Education. He entitled his comments "Teaching is Living." Yes, his comments had been used before because this thought was the most important thing in the whole realm of education as far as William Henry Oliver was concerned. (Henry Oliver, January 15 and August 22, 1968, Oliver Collection)

Mr. Oliver submitted his request to retire from Belmont in 1970. He thought Belmont was a good school and he was happy there. But just as his retirement from public schools had not been final retirement, so his retirement from Belmont was not to be his final retirement either.

> . . . As prospective teachers from Free Will Baptist Bible College kept coming to . . . Belmont to complete their requirements for teacher certification, there began to grow . . . a feeling that the teacher training program at Free Will Baptist Bible College ought to be expanded and that I might be a part of it. So I wrote Dr. Johnson a letter offering my services and here I am. (Jean Picirilli, editor, *Lumen*, 1975)

Many years had passed since William Henry Oliver had taught in a Free Will Baptist school, but the pendulum had swung back and in 1970, he was "back where he started." In the announcement of his appointment to teach in the fields of Education and English, there is a summary of his career. He was an ordained Free Will Baptist minister who had worked for thirty-four years as a teacher, principal, and superintendent of schools in the Nashville public school system. He had been an Associate Professor of Education at Belmont College. (*Free Will Baptist Bible College Bulletin*, August, 1970) Shortly after the opening of the school year, he spoke in chapel about his experiences "From Eureka to F.W.B.B.C." (Henry Oliver, September, 1970, Oliver Collection) Bro. Oliver told Dr. L.C. Johnson, President of the college, that it was a fulfillment of his original dream. (Dr. L.C. Johnson to the author, June 12, 1975) Remember, his dream had been to serve his denominational school. Bro. Oliver spoke in chapel in 1971, entitling his remarks "Reflections, Comparisons, and Impressions." He took a backward glance at his sixty-one years of experience in education before coming to Free Will Baptist Bible College. He commented on the modest dress of the students, the fact that the school had a purpose, and that the faculty was a team who loved God.

Who could speak at the faculty meeting on "Teacher-Student Relationships"? If anyone was qualified, it was Bro. Oliver. Thus, it was he who talked to his fellow workers in 1971. It sounded like some of his former speeches to teachers when he mentioned that they were leaders and probably the best persons some students had ever known. It was different though when he referred to seeking always the guidance of the Holy Spirit. Teachers in Christian schools should be called and commissioned by God Himself. (Henry Oliver, January 8 and April 12, 1971, Oliver Collection)

Bro. Oliver's article, "Flowing and Growing," referred to Eureka as the stream of Free Will Baptist education running underground." He wrote, "I have again found at least a part of the main stream of Free Will Baptist education. It has surfaced magnificently and is now a steady river, not as big as it will someday be, but growing constantly as it makes its way on down the valley of Christian service. I have returned to the work to which I have always felt that God originally called me." He described the students, the teachers, the curriculum, and the facilities at the college. In conclusion,

> We have not yet become all that we hope to be. We want to reach more students. We want to train more Christian workers. There are still other courses to be added and perhaps higher plateaus of accreditation to be reached, but Free Will Baptist Bible College is a good school, worthy of the prayers and support of all Christians . . . .The stream of Free Will Baptist Christian education hardly deserves even yet to be called a mighty river, but it has surfaced and it is flowing and growing. I do not believe that it will ever go underground again. (*Free Will Baptist Bible College Bulletin,* March/April, 1971)

With a chuckle, Mr. Oliver said "They have even asked me to speak at graduation once since I've been back." So in 1971, he talked about the world the graduates were entering. Our nation was at war in Vietnam. Fears of inflation, unemployment, and economic depression were prevalent. "We are becoming a bureaucracy controlled by boards and committees with a tendency toward socialism and an apathy even toward creeping communism . . . ." He called the new morality a reversion to immorality, which is not new. "Religion is the mother of education; the church is the parent of the school. And now education, like a rebellious teenage child, is saying to religion, its parent, 'We have no further need of you'." He mentioned taking Bible reading and prayer out of public schools. He stated that he was thankful for the Christian schools springing up all over the country. America was built upon the foundations of her homes, schools, and churches. With these crumbling, one could no longer say the United States was a God-fearing, Christian nation. He went further to challenge his listeners.

> Please do not go into this world with a feeling of . . . defeatism . . . for this world which has so much wrong with it is also a world of great opportunity . . . . Ours is the great commission to go into all the world and preach the Gospel to every creature, teaching them to observe all things whatsoever He has commanded you and He has promised to be with you even to the end of the world . . . . Be of good cheer. Christ, your Christ, has overcome the world. Be of good cheer! (Henry Oliver, May 14, 1971, Oliver Collection)

In his third year at the college, Bro. Oliver was the sponsor for the Freshman Class. When he spoke to them, he mentioned all the things any class sponsor would, including extracurricular activities, school work, finances, and future plans. He went on to speak of the importance of a strong faith, their prayer life, and Bible reading habits. (Henry Oliver, 1972, Oliver Collection)

William Henry Oliver gave the opening address at the Principals' Conference in 1972 on the campus of Free Will Baptist Bible College. Principals of Free Will Baptist elementary and secondary schools from several states attended. His address was entitled "Private Church Related

Schools in American Education—Past, Present, and Future." Church schools were nothing new on the American scene. Religious motivation brought about the first legislation requiring schools. This was done in the seventeenth century by the Puritans in Massachusetts. Education was born in America as the child of the church. Professor Oliver summarized the fight for public education, the progress and success of public schools. For years, these schools emphasized biblical principles. When this ceased to exist, reasons were evident for church schools again. Thus, the present Christian education movement blossomed. Professor Oliver listed the following reasons under "Why Christian Day Schools?" (1) Public schools are without religion. (2) They have loose morals. (3) There is permissive conduct and lack of discipline. (4) The work is superficial. (5) School pride has been lost. (6) Some teachers are not Christians. (7) Public schools are ignoring the wishes of parents. Professor Oliver also talked about the difficulties of the church-related schools. These included competition with affluent public schools, finances, buildings, equipment, finding well-qualified and available teachers, and accreditation. What of the future? Professor Oliver stated, "I just don't know. Only God knows." He used this material again with a class he taught in 1973. (Henry Oliver, October 5, 1972 and April 18, 1973, Oliver Collection)

On the second day of the Principals' Conference, Bro. Oliver spoke on a familiar topic for him, "Teaching by Example." He called teaching by personal example the most effective method of teaching, whether inside or outside the classroom. The objective of a teacher is the development, improvement, education, and progress of human beings. It is not the dissemination of subject matter. Whether it be to the advantage or disadvantage of their students, every teacher teaches by example. What one professes is of little importance compared to what one practices. "Strive to make as effective as possible your personal influence, and make sure that your example will be a safe one to copy." He then called to their attention specific aspects in which they were to be examples. He listed scholarship, citizenship, optimism, moral and spiritual living, and philosophy of life. The following year Bro. Oliver used these same notes at Woodbine Christian Academy's In-Service. (Henry Oliver, October 6, 1972 and April 17, 1973, Oliver Collection)

"Facing the Future" was Professor Oliver's topic in chapel at Free Will Baptist Bible College in 1972. He challenged students to face the future unafraid, walking close to God. "Advance in the future with the idea of serving rather than being served." (Henry Oliver, November 3, 1972, Oliver Collection) Professor Oliver spoke in chapel on another occasion when he commended the students and faculty. He stated, "I am a judge of schools and teachers." Certainly, nobody doubted that. He challenged students to prepare for the work God had for each to do. (Henry Oliver, January 24, 1974, Oliver Collection)

The editor of the 1973 *Lumen*, Free Will Baptist Bible College's yearbook, asked the right person to write about the Christian virtue of gentleness. The *Lumen* featured articles about several virtues. Professor Oliver wrote that the word "gentleness" is one of the most beautiful and poetic words in our language. The "gentleness of Christ" is referred to in II Corinthians 10:1. It is one of the fruits of the Spirit listed in Galatians 5:22. He wrote about the words "gentle and gently." Professor Oliver closed the article with, "Gentleness, I repeat, is derived from love and is kindness in action." (Henry Oliver, November 15, 1972, Oliver Collection)

Professor Oliver spoke at Woodbine Christian Academy's In-Service again in 1974. He entitled his remarks simply "Discipline." He covered three main areas. These included the causes of misbehavior, achieving classroom control, and creating self-discipline. His advice was to have a few definite rules and enforce them. Punishment should be rare but when necessary, swift and certain. (Henry Oliver, January 24 and August 29, 1974, Oliver Collection)

Professor Oliver went to the National Free Will Baptist Headquarters to bring a devotion. Using several passages in Psalms including 102:25-27, he shared thoughts on "Man's Refuge—Trusting in Time of Fear." Again, this was used on other occasions. (Henry Oliver, January 24, August 29 and October 9, 1974, Oliver Collection)

> The most vital link in Free Will Baptist Bible College's chain is her teachers. Teachers dedicated to God—their students—education—right. One such man has dedicated his whole life to education. And why? He loves God—his students—education—right. Because of this love, dedication and loyalty exemplify his life as an educator, the 1975 *Lumen* staff wishes to recognize such unfailing loyalty to God and education in the only way we know how. (Jean Picirilli, editor, *Lumen*, 1975)

So reads the dedication of the 1975 *Lumen* to Professor William Henry Oliver. The editor presented the first copy to Professor Oliver in chapel shortly before the closing of the spring semester. The professor had been known to serenade his English classes with his harmonica.

Thus, the *Lumen* staff thought it appropriate to give him a new one. To show his appreciation for yet another honor, he performed on his new harmonica for the faculty and student body. (*Free Will Baptist Bible College Bulletin*, May/June, 1975) Included in the *Lumen* was Professor Oliver's article on "Called to Teach." He believed that just as surely as God called him to preach and sing, God called him to teach. Having done all three, God had graciously blessed in all three activities. In conclusion, "The students at Free Will Baptist Bible College are the finest group of young people that I have ever known. I hope that God will call many of them to teach." (Jean Picirilli, editor, *Lumen*, 1975) Rick Rasberry, a student at the time, said they had an unusual chapel. "Everybody loved that man."(Rick Rasberry to the author, spring, 1975)

Little has been said about the classes Professor Oliver taught at the college or his actual work. The Provost at Welch College, (formerly Free Will Baptist Bible College) Dr. Greg Ketteman, had Professor Oliver for English in 1973. He says of Mr. Oliver that he was one of the most generous, gracious men he ever met. Mr. Oliver was a true Christian gentleman. Dr. Ketteman spent thirty years in Metro schools and he commented on the impact Mr. Oliver had before his days at the Free Will Baptist College. As superintendent, Mr. Oliver preferred to hire Christians who influenced students in public schools for years after he was superintendent. Henry Oliver's legacy continues as many in Nashville and Davidson County remember this beloved man. One man can make an impact! (Greg Ketteman to the author, October 20, 2015)

Mr. Oliver taught both inside and outside the classroom. The Dean of the School of Education at Trevecca

Nazarene University said, "So much of what he shared with me influenced my life forever. I learned so much about teaching from my kind and caring professor . . . in his class. Outside of the classroom, I learned about the beauty of our Father's world as I listened to Mr. Oliver relive touching stories of his childhood, his family, his ministry, his teaching career, and his tenure as superintendent of schools. . . ."

Many students can recall how Mr. Oliver continued to encourage and inspire years after they were in his classes. Here is just one example. "Mr. Oliver was my mentor as I struggled as a new teacher in those early years to effectively reach my students. He was instrumental in opening my eyes to the needs of the precious lives the Lord had placed within my hands. Even when I took a break from teaching, Mr. Oliver continued to be an inspiration and a source of encouragement to me as I worked as a free-lance artist and greeting card writer. My pen name was Oliver James." (Dr. Suzie Barker Harris to the author, March 9, 2016)

What were his contributions in the education department? He helped develop the Teacher Training Program and many courses were added in the college catalog. "We have used his experience, his judgment, his strengths, and the weight of his own personality . . . He is popular with students and respected highly." (Dr. L.C. Johnson to the author, June 12, 1975) In Professor Oliver's own words,

> There has been great expansion of our program in teacher training . . . both in courses offered and in faculty members. I am proud of our department of education and of our entire faculty and staff . . . . We are

preparing . . . workers for a field in which the demand for Christian service is especially great at the present time and in the immediate future.   Very many of our students are . . . the kind of Christians whom God can use in the profession of teaching. (Jean Picirilli, editor, *Lumen*, 1975)

Henry Oliver said he had not finished his work at Free Will Baptist College. He planned to return to teaching in the fall of 1975, "the Lord willing." He did so and continued to teach until 1977. ("Former Teacher With The Lord," *Free Will Baptist Bible College Bulletin*, May/June 1991)

What a special occasion for the author in the spring of 1977! She was present at Free Will Baptist Bible College as the first copy of the original <u>Founded Upon a Rock</u> was presented to Mr. Oliver. With his characteristic humility, he accepted the book as students and faculty honored him with applause and a standing ovation.

In August of 1977, Pauline Oliver left this earthly life. Saddened though he was by his wife's passing, Henry Oliver continued to faithfully serve until his own death in 1991.

Thus far, this book has largely been a summary of William Henry Oliver's life's work with occasional references to other activities. Though Mr. Oliver went beyond the call of duty in his vocation, he also found time to devote to worthwhile causes and organizations. The reader is asked to turn your attention to some of these activities.

Mr. Oliver was the father of the YMCA (Young Men's Christian Association) Branch in East Nashville and instrumental in organizing the East Center where he was a charter member of the Board. East was the first center in Nashville. He was a part of the group that conceived of Community YMCA Programs. This group interviewed and employed Comer Teal as Nashville's first Community Program Director. Mr. Oliver served on many of this Board's committees and as Chairman of the Board for two terms in the second and third years of its existence. He was the Secretary-Treasurer during the YMCA's first year. Mr. Oliver was the principal speaker at East YMCA's First Annual Progress Report Dinner Meeting. Henry Oliver was a strong supporter and worker in the Capital Funds Campaign leading to the construction of the new Family YMCA Building on Gallatin Road. The East Center, under his philosophy, became the first Family YMCA in Nashville and one of the first in the country. Each year a Special Community-YMCA Service Award is given to an individual who has made outstanding contributions to the Nashville Community and the YMCA. "NOW, THEREFORE, BE IT RESOLVED that WILLIAM HENRY OLIVER be awarded the YMCA'S SPECIAL SERVICE PLAQUE." This plaque was presented on May 13, 1975 at the Hillwood Country Club at the Association's 100th Annual meeting and Awards Banquet. George H. Cate, Jr., a former student of Mr. Oliver's and a Nashville attorney, presented the plaque. As an admirer said, "Mr. William Henry Oliver has indeed left a great mark for good on his community and is highly deserving of this Award." (The plaque along with other information was found in the Oliver Collection)

In 1975, Mr. Oliver received his twenty-five year pin from the American Red Cross. He was also president of the

Nashville Civitans and a thirty-third degree Mason, one of only about fifty in Tennessee at that time. (Henry Oliver to the author, July 9, 1975) He was invited by Fulton Edwards, Worshipful Master, to speak at the Masonic Centennial at Indian Mound in 1966. He always welcomed an opportunity to go "home" to Stewart County. In his speech on "The Masonic Home," he made it exceedingly clear that the home is the key to a nation's greatness. Mr. Oliver served as chapter advisor for De Molay and participated in many programs of the Rainbows. He spoke to the Eastern Star on a number of occasions. (Henry Oliver, October 8, 1966, Oliver Collection)

Chapter Three captured some of Rev. Oliver's messages at homecomings at Dunbar's Chapel. He was often a guest speaker at other church homecomings. In 1964 he spoke on "What is your Relationship to God?" at Indian Mound United Methodist Church. (Henry Oliver, Summer, 1964, Oliver Collection) East Nashville Free Will Baptist Church had a "Beginners' Homecoming" in 1958 centered around the theme "Training the Child." Ones who had been in the Beginners Class many years before participated as well as some of the Beginners in 1958. Since Rev. Oliver was the pastor when the class was organized, he brought a devotion on "Training the Child." (Henry Oliver, February 9, 1958, Oliver Collection) Horton Heights Free Will Baptist Church heard Rev. Oliver at their homecoming in 1965. His morning message was entitled "Three Kinds of Homecomings." (Henry Oliver, September 12 1965, Oliver Collection) Rev. Oliver was the pastor of Bethlehem Free Will Baptist Church near Ashland City in 1933. The church asked him to preach at their 1972 homecoming. He used John 3:16 and Luke 15 for his Scripture text. (Henry Oliver, May 7, 1972, Oliver Collection)

Rather than attempting to cover all Rev. Oliver's speaking appointments at East Nashville Free Will Baptist Church, some remarks about East's "Golden Anniversary" are included here. Bro. Oliver brought the message on September 14, 1973 as that day was the "Kick-Off" for a year-long anniversary celebration. It was only natural that Rev. Oliver serve as Chairman. This committee compiled the *Golden Memory Book* in an effort to recapture the first fifty years. The book was dedicated to the memory of Fannie Polston's undaunted faith, personal dedication and love for the Lord. William Henry Oliver is listed as the pastor from September of 1924 until October of 1926 and again from October of 1934 until May of 1935. "Occasionally Brother William Henry Oliver, first pastor and charter member of the church sings a solo, as he has been doing for fifty years." On "Anniversary Sunday," September 8, 1974, the charter members blew out fifty candles on a huge birthday cake. Rev. J.L. Welch, former pastor and organizer of the church, was the speaker of the day. Special music was rendered in the evening by Henry Oliver and his brother John, and L.G. Ennis. (*Golden Memory Book*, 1974, a part of the Oliver Collection)

On at least three occasions since Mr. Oliver left East High as the principal, he delivered the Baccalaureate sermon at the school. Once he spoke on "Faith," as there was no topic which could be more profitable to think on for that hour. (Henry Oliver, June 1, 1958, Oliver Collection) He chose for his topic in 1961 "Putting First Things First." A few months later, he used these notes when he preached at the Negro Church of God Convention. (Henry Oliver, May 29 and August 16, 1961, Oliver Collection) Two years later he went back to East as the Baccalaureate speaker, using a favorite address on "What is Your Relationship to God?"

The students at Hume-Fogg's Baccalaureate heard the same question as did those at Cumberland High School. (Henry Oliver, June 2, 1963, May 31, 1964 and May 31, 1965, Oliver Collection)

"Success in Any Career" was an appropriate title for a Commencement Address. Professor Oliver used these notes at Austin Peay State University's Career Day and for the commencement address at W.T. Thomas High School in Cumberland City, Tennessee, at David Lipscomb High School, and at Mt. Olive (North Carolina) Junior College. Professor Oliver was especially glad to go back to Eastern North Carolina where he had spent some time in his early years. He declined the offer to become the Dean at this college when he was at Belmont because of so many ties in Nashville. His words there varied some from his usual "Success in Any Career." The key words he used were man, heroes, giants, and God. Among his notes were the poems "If" by Rudyard Kipling, "Excelsior" and "A Psalm of Life" by Henry W. Longfellow and "God, Give Us Men" by Josiah Gilbert Holland. (Henry Oliver, April 27, 1961, May 21 and June 4, 1965, June 6, 1966, Oliver Collection) Henry Oliver was present at Stewart County High School's graduation in 1969 where he graciously made a few remarks when asked. (Henry Oliver, May 22, 1969, Oliver Collection)

Dedications are invariably occasions for speakers to wax eloquent. William Henry Oliver was on hand to make remarks at quite a few. The Reed-Cox Memorial Chapel on the campus of Tennessee Tech in Cookeville, Tennessee was dedicated as a part of the Wesley Foundation Methodist Student Center. It was named in honor of James Hugh Reed and Mrs. Ethel Reed Cox. Mr. Oliver was one of three people who gave "Personal Tributes." (Henry Oliver, December 13,

1959, Oliver Collection) Superintendent of Nashville Schools, Mr. Henry Oliver, presented an appropriate Dedication Address at Bellwood Elementary School in Murfreesboro, Tennessee. It was indeed a long way from McGregor School to Bellwood as Mr. Oliver pointed out. Yet, the essential elements of learning were still the same. (Henry Oliver, May 26, 1963, Oliver Collection) John Oliver, Henry's brother, was the principal of West High School when the W.H. Yarbrough Gymnasium was dedicated. Professor William Henry Oliver of Belmont College delivered the Dedication Address. The opposing team to play that night, ironically, was the East High Eagles. Twenty-five years earlier Mr. Oliver made some remarks at the dedication of the football stadium at West. Again, ironically, the opposing team that night was East. Mr. Oliver's wish was still the same. It was that good sportsmanship prevail always and that "may you never be beaten . . . by an inferior team. It is no disgrace to lose to a team that is better . . . . " (Henry Oliver, November 28, 1954, Oliver Collection) "Greatness" was Mr. Oliver's topic at the dedication of the John F. Kennedy Band Room at the Washington Junior High School. (Henry Oliver, May 3, 1965, Oliver Collection)

Mr. Oliver was first an American but he was also a Southerner. At least twice he addressed the Daughters of the American Revolution. He talked about the Constitution to the French Lick chapter in Scott's Hill, Tennessee. He gave a speech on the "Difficulties of War for Independence" to the Nashville chapter. (Henry Oliver, September 14, 1968 and February 22, 1973, Oliver Collection) Mr. Oliver spoke in memory of Sam Davis to the United Daughters of the Confederacy meeting at the Sam Davis Home in Smyrna, Tennessee. The Vanderbilt Dames heard him speak on "The

Face of the South," which he described as a beautiful, sad, sweet, and happy face. Professor Oliver addressed the Mt. Olivet Confederate Circle at a Memorial Service in the Mt. Olivet Cemetery to honor all Confederate dead and to pay special tribute to Jefferson Davis. (Henry Oliver, May 31, 1958, February 8, 1961 and June 6, 1965, Oliver Collection)

Mr. Oliver spoke to the Jaycees, the Lions, Business and Professional Women, Senior Citizens, and Breakfast Clubs. He once spoke to the Tennessee Bureau for Lathing and Plastering. Twice he addressed Beta Club Conventions. Going through Mr. Oliver's notes for speeches was indeed an experience!

During the last eleven years covered by the original book, Mr. Oliver was honored and praised by many groups as well as individuals. This chapter has only scratched the surface. There is no further need to comment on his accomplishments.

From 1977 until his passage into His Savior's presence on May 15, 1991, William Henry Oliver handled what came his way as he always had, with a strong faith and a positive outlook on life. Always a lover of poetry, here is one of his little favorites.

Don't look for the flaws as you go through life;

And even when you find them,

It is wise and kind to be somewhat blind,

And look for the good behind them.

"I still have trouble with my feet. Walking is slow, somewhat staggery, and painful. Otherwise I am doing fine." (Henry Oliver to the author, November 3, 1981) "My health is greatly improved but I still have difficulty walking." However, he was planning to visit the World's Fair in Knoxville that summer. (Henry Oliver to the author, May 10, 1982) His walking improved but he still used a cane. For his birthday in 1985, the author took Bro. Oliver to Stewart County. As he walked around in the Seay Cemetery at Indian Mound, he commented that most of his friends were now on the other side. As his eyes roamed the rolling hills on the way to Dunbar's Chapel, he quoted poetry he had memorized as a student in Stewart County. He pointed out as near as possible the site of McGregor School from the road. It was on to Dover with a visit to the Brutons and to Oakwood to see the Morelands. Indeed, it was a memorable day for both Bro. Oliver and the author. (Personal memories of the author) "I'm not complaining. I am very thankful to be as well off as I am. Life has been very good to me and I regard every additional year of life as a generous bonus from God and I pray that I may live each day in a way that will please Him." (Henry Oliver to the author, Christmastime, 1988) He had angina for several years before he had open heart surgery. He told the author that he would call 911, pack his little suitcase and sit on the porch waiting for the paramedics to arrive and transport him to the hospital. (Personal memories of the author) Always one to help others, he had a couple and their children who lived with him for a time. "I told Wayne after Miriam's death that he and the children could stay in my home until they could do better. I can give them food and shelter. I am glad to do this for Miriam, who was one of my finest and dearest students. The children are in school at Woodbine and Wayne is working part time at a machine shop."(Henry Oliver to the author, October 31, 1986)

Through physical ailments that came in his later years, Henry Oliver still showed the character he had demonstrated over his entire life. He continued to show appreciation to those who remembered him and expressed an interest in what others were doing. "I greatly appreciated your letter. . . I greatly enjoyed having your mother and Marlene visit me. . . I congratulate you on being principal . . . I would like to know about your school. . . . How far along are you with your doctorate? . . . I wish you God's blessings." In a postscript, he mentioned that the couple staying with him were doing an excellent job in taking care of him. (Henry Oliver to the author, October 19, 1987)

Henry Oliver sent a typed Christmas letter in 1988. He left a blank where he wrote the name of the recipient. Although his wish was to send a personal letter to each individual expressing his thanks, it was impractical because of too many friends. Besides, "the facility with which I could write in former years is no longer with me." He still received about 200 Christmas cards each year. He was not alone for a young married couple from Free Will Baptist College lived with him. He considered them to be a part of his household. "They take good care of me—my meals, my medication, my clothes, etc. I am very fortunate to have them." He could no longer drive because of his vision. Hazel, John's wife, took him to church. His brother and sister, Herschel and Pearl, took turns taking him to the doctor's lab each Monday. Barbara Morgan, a former student, took him to the Civitan luncheon on Tuesdays, for haircuts, to the funeral homes and anywhere else he needed to go. Price Carney took him to Chamber of Commerce meetings. "Everyone is very kind to me." He concluded by wishing a Christmas season of joy, Christian peace and contentment and a New Year of health, happiness and prosperity to those who received this letter. He signed off with "Sincerely, gratefully and prayerfully." The signature still looked very much like it had for many years. He wrote a personal note, "Hope to see you while you are at home." (Henry Oliver to the author, Christmastime, 1988)

The author last saw Bro. Oliver in the summer of 1990 or 19991. She and her Mother visited him in his home on Eastland Avenue. He was in a hospital bed at that time, still mentally alert and a pleasure to visit. On his wall hung a picture of a winter scene of Indian Mound painted by Alberta Tippit. Yes, Stewart County and those he knew there were always with him.

The evidence has been presented to verify the fact that his life is "liken . . . unto a wise man, which built his house upon a rock: And the rain descended, and the floods came, and the winds blew, and beat upon that house; and it fell not: for it was **FOUNDED UPON A ROCK**." (Matthew 7:24b-25.)

Mr. Oliver and the author, Belmont, May, 1970

Marlene (Edwards) Tidwell and Mr. Oliver, Free Will Baptist Bible College, May, 1980

These photos are in the author's collection.

Jean Picirilli, editor of the 1975 *Lumen*, presented the first copy to Mr. Oliver to whom it was dedicated.

Photo in the *Free Will Baptist Bible College Bulletin*, May/June of 1975

Iris D. Charton and William Henry Oliver, Associate
Professors of Education at Belmont

Photo in the 1969 *Tower*

Dr. Dale E. Young | 187
Founded Upon A Rock

(Top) Dunbar's Chapel Homecoming where Bro. Oliver enjoyed "dinner on the ground" in July of 1972. (Bottom) Dunbar's Chapel Homecoming with Jason Edwards, July of 1976

Claude Adams with Henry Oliver at Dunbar's Chapel Homecoming, July of 1980

Henry Oliver with his sisters, Myrtle Stanley and Pearl Miller, at Dunbar's Chapel Homecoming, July of 1987

Mr. Oliver presented the Civitan Award at Woodbine Christian Academy in 1986. Left to Right: Mr. Oliver, Michael Curtis, and the author. Michael's Dad was a graduate of East Nashville High School. That's Michael's little brother in the background.

These photos are in the author's collection.

CHAPTER 7

THE AFTERGLOW

An afterglow is a reflection of past success, a glow remaining where a light has disappeared. "When the sun goes below the horizon he is not set; the heavens glow for a full hour after his departure. And when a great and good man sets, the sky of this world is luminous long after he is out of sight. Such a man cannot die out of this world. When he goes he leaves behind him much of himself. Being dead, he speaks." (Lyman Beecher as quoted in <u>Streams in the Desert, Vol. I</u>, compiled by Mrs. Charles E. Cowen, c. 1925, p. 164) Based on the impact and influence William Henry Oliver had in many areas and on many lives, this is a fitting way to close this work.

William Henry Oliver, age 87, departed this life May 15, 1991 from the Helen Pate-Bain Health Care Center. He returned one last time to the school he so lovingly nurtured years before. It came as no surprise that he had planned his own service, specifically requesting that the service "not be excessively long." His pastor from East Nashville Free Will Baptist Church, Fred Hall, and Drs. L.C. Johnson and Charles Thigpen, both of whom served as president of Free Will Baptist Bible College, honored his request as they officiated for the funeral lasted less than an hour. Memorial contributions were to go to Free Will Baptist Bible College or the William Henry Oliver Scholarship Fund through the East High School Alumni Association. Reverend Henry Oliver, educator and minister, was laid to rest beside his beloved wife whom he fondly called "Polly" in Forest Lawn Memorial Gardens on May 18, 1991. So much for what sounded like a typical obituary; this servant's funeral was not typical. In attendance were former Mayor Richard Fulton, Mayor Bill Boner, hundreds of former students, co-workers and acquaintances from all walks of life. Obituaries listed many organizations and honors which have been mentioned in other chapters of this book. (Sources of obituaries included the *Free Will Baptist Bible College Bulletin, Contact, The Eagle, Nashville Banner and Tennessean*)

Prior to his funeral, an editorial had said about Mr. Oliver: "The officials and citizens throughout the nation who are now debating ways to improve education could take some lessons from Mr. William Henry Oliver. There are literally thousands of people—many of them leaders in this community—who remember Mr. Oliver's gentle and caring way with young people. He didn't simply educate, he inspired. And his inspiration will continue in the hearts of all who knew him." (*The Tennessean*, May 18, 1991) What a tribute!

Suzie and Dale Harris sat with their children, Christopher and AnnaGee, behind Tennessee's poet laureate, Peck Gunn, at Mr. Oliver's funeral. As this family left the service, Pearl Oliver Miller recognized AnnaGee and stepped out of the limousine, extended her loving arms to AnnaGee, and they wept together. A week later, Pearl gave Suzie a box of letters Suzie had written to Mr. Oliver. The cards and letters dated from 1974 to 1990 and chronicled her life as a student at Free Will Baptist Bible College, a wife, mother, and teacher. "Knowing my beloved teacher, Mr. Oliver, kept my letters throughout the years brought great comfort to me." He had sung "Oh Perfect Love" at her wedding and there in the box she found her wedding invitation, birth announcements of her children, and letters the children wrote recapping their visits with Mr. Oliver both in his home and theirs. When they visited, he told stories about fox hunting with their great grandfather, Cotton Harris. "Such visits greatly impacted both of the children; . . . AnnaGee, still carries . . . a deep love for literature and the fine arts, which I contribute to her first introduction to 'Jenny Kiss'd Me' recited to her . . . by Mr. Oliver. . . I take the letters out from time to time and am reminded of what an impact this precious teacher had on my life." (Dr. Suzie Barker Harris to the author, March 9, 2016)

Bob Bosworth, Bruno as many called him, was the drum major at East High School and a member of the Class of 1952. He wrote about Mr. Oliver in the East Nashville High Alumni Association's paper.

> ...I was always impressed with what he remembered about me and how he could always place me on a higher plane than I actually was . . . he was a man among men, and one who never took his

role in life lightly... Some... refer to it as the funeral ... but I would like to think of it as Mr. Oliver's Homegoing. It was as if Mr. Oliver himself had called an assembly . . . and all his students had answered the call. You could look around . . . and see classes gathering . . . renewing old acquaintances. Remembering moments of the past . . . people who were no longer here. . . the good times and the bad . . . The day we had all known was coming, but hated to see. The day we would say goodbye to Mr. Oliver. ... We were told that Mr. Oliver himself had written the instructions and the services were to be brief. As the eulogies began, it was evident, each person had his or her own special memory to relive, for the man who had been so many things to so many different people. ...words were always a great part of Mr. Oliver's life, his music was shared equally. (Bob Bosworth, "Mr. Oliver Remembered," *The Eagle*, January, 1992)

Songs of praise and dedication filled the air. Mr. Fred Waller sang "My Task" to those gathered. The song brought to mind the times Mr. Oliver sang to students as he encouraged them over the years. (Corinne Wright to the author, July 29, 2015)

> To love someone more dearly ev'ry day
> To help a wand'ring child to find his way
> To ponder o'er a noble tho't and pray
> And smile when evening falls
> And smile when evening falls
> This is my task

> To follow truth as blind me long for light
> To do my best from dawn of day till night
> To keep my heart fit for His holy sight
> And answer when He calls
> And answer when He calls
> This is my task
>
>
> And then my Savior by and by to meet
> When faith hath made her task on earth complete
> And lay my homage at the Master's feet
> Within the jasper walls
> Within the jasper walls
> This crowns my task.

(E.L. Ashford, "To Love Someone More Dearly" or "My Task," words public domain)

As the echoes of this song drifted from the podium through the rows across the auditorium, Mr. Oliver was there in many ways. Love and death create a bond. Those present had to come to grips with a beginning and an end that day. This man had guided the lives of the former students only for a brief time but he had infused a "certain something" in them. He was gone from their midst and they were sad. As it was ending and people began to file out, smiles crossed their faces as "Pomp and Circumstance" began to play. Bob exclaimed to a friend standing by him, "Mr. Oliver just graduated, didn't he? (Bob Bosworth, "Mr. Oliver Remembered," *The Eagle*, January, 1992)

The funeral procession then winded its way to Forest Lawn Memorial Gardens. "I will never forget the funeral procession of William Henry Oliver on that warm May afternoon in 1991." The line seemed endless as countless devoted students, friends, and family members drove slowly in the procession. On the side of the road, two teenage boys stood at attention by their bicycles with their ball caps placed over their hearts. "What a fitting tribute to this beautiful man of God, this wonderful educator who made such a difference in the lives of so many, many students." (Dr. Suzie Barker Harris to the author, March 9, 2016)

Men are honored by having their name on buildings, scholarships and various other things. The William Henry Oliver Scholarship honors this man and is awarded annually to direct descendants of an East High graduate who is a member in good standing with the East Nashville High Alumni Association. Recipients may be graduates of East Nashville Magnet High School or other schools or a graduating Senior of East Nashville Magnet School. To fund this scholarship, the alumni association hosts an annual golf tournament with all proceeds going into the scholarship fund. The scholarships in 2014 totaled $12,000 and in 2015 totaled $11,000. (Joanna Blackwell to the author, June 22, 2015) Stewart County High School gave scholarships bearing Mr. Oliver's name for a number of years but doesn't do so now. One school bears the name of William Henry Oliver, the middle school located at 6211 Nolensville Road in Nashville.

On May 18, 2014, Dunbar's Chapel celebrated their 100th anniversary. It was the author's privilege to share the church history, much of which had been provided by William Henry Oliver. Pleasant memories brought mental pictures to mind as stories he told were recalled. Both tears and chuckles came as the congregation reminisced. Bro.

Oliver was then with his Savior but the lives of those present had been touched by this servant of God.

"Who will take their places?" was a question Henry Oliver asked at Dunbar's Chapel homecoming. (Henry Oliver, "Homecoming at Dunbar's Chapel," July 26, 1964)

> After I leave for worlds unknown,
>
> Over the border line;
>
> Never again on earth to roam,
>
> What will I leave behind?
>
> Leave behind, yes, Leave behind,
>
> What will I leave behind?
>
> After I leave for worlds unknown,
>
> What will I leave behind?

(Sherrill Brown, "What Will I Leave Behind?", c. 1958 by Stamps Quartet Music Company)

This last chapter attempted to answer the question of what did William Henry Oliver leave behind. Truly, he left a godly legacy. Reader, consider are you taking a place which William Henry Oliver would consider worthwhile?

This bronze monument marks the final resting place of the Oliver's in Forest Lawn Memorial Gardens. He often signed off using his initials which are imbedded on the photo.

Photo from Corinne Wright